Windows NT™
Registry
Guide

Weiying Chen
Wayne Berry

ADDISON-WESLEY DEVELOPERS PRESS

An imprint of Addison Wesley Longman, Inc.

Reading, Massachusetts • Harlow, England • Menlo Park, California
Berkeley, California • Don Mills, Ontario • Sydney
Bonn • Amsterdam • Tokyo • Mexico City

Library of Congress Cataloging-in-Publication Data

Chen, Weiying.
   Windows NT Registry guide / Weiying Chen, Wayne Berry. p.   cm.
   Includes index.
   ISBN 0-201-69473-5
   1. Microsoft Windows NT. 2. Operating systems (Computers)
I. Berry, Wayne. II. Title.
QA76.76.063C4577 1997
005.4'469—dc21   96-29753
                                                                 CIP

Sponsoring Editor: Mary Treseler
Project Manager: Sarah Weaver
Cover Design: Ann Gallager
Cover Photograph: Eric Wessman, Photonica
Set in 10-point Palatino by CIP of Coronado

1 2 3 4 5 6 7 8 9 -MA- 0100999897
First printing, May 1997

Addison Wesley Longman, Inc., books are available for bulk purchases by corporations, institutions, and other organizations. For more information please contact the Corporate, Government, and Special Sales Department at (800) 238-9682.

Find A-W Developers Press on the World Wide Web at
http://www.aw.com/devpress/

Contents

Acknowledgments

First, I would like to thank a couple of people at Addison-Wesley: Mary Treseler, sponsoring editor, who gave me this opportunity, and the project manager, Sarah Weaver, who managed the production of this book.

I would also like to thank my parents (Chuanzhong Chen and Chayun Qian), my sister (Xiaoping Chen), and my friends Hong Zhao and Biffle French, who gave me constant encouragement. Thanks are also due to Martin Kohlleppel, who has provided much valuable feedback and has been very supportive throughout the many long evenings and weekends I spent on this book.

Weiying Chen

Introduction

The **Registry** is a central storage location that is part of the Windows NT 4.0 operating system. It contains state and configuration information about a computer and its applications and operating system. It also contains information about the computer's user.

Although seemingly only a simple indexed database, the Registry is actually a very powerful resource originally designed to be used only by the operating system and other applications. It was never intended to be accessed by a user. Some people may disagree with this last statement. However, we offer the following arguments to support this view:

- No applications for viewing or modifying the Registry are visible on the Desktop. A Registry Editor is shipped with Windows NT and Windows 95, but no icon for it is placed on the Desktop, on the task bar, or even in the Control Panel. This seems to indicate that the user is not supposed to know about or use the Registry.

- The programming APIs to the Registry are more involved and better than the Registry Editor. This indicates that it is more important for programs to use the Registry than for a user to access it.

We feel that users were never intended to use the Registry because *modification of the Registry could destroy the operating system.* And destroying the operating system is the worst thing a user can do to a computer through software. The system can be recovered only by reinstalling it, plus all applications that had run on it. For this reason, we strongly urge you to back up your computer's Registry *before* you begin to implement any of the procedures and suggestions we offer in this book. Instructions for doing this are in Chapter 1.

Because the Registry seems to be inaccessible, it may appear to users to be a mysterious place full of secrets. It's not. Editing the Registry is easy, much like using Explorer to edit files. And programming it is straightforward, similar to using Microsoft Foundation Classes. The only real mystery involved is the information it contains. And in this book, we help you sort through that.

Use of the Registry to store state information is growing in popularity for several reasons:

- As software companies upgrade their applications, they are changing their state saving mechanism from .ini files to the Registry. Since the number of software companies is increasing and the Registry is the "place to be," there will be more application development that incorporates the Registry.

- As PCs grow more powerful, they are increasingly being used as servers. However, most servers have limited graphical user interfaces. Hence, the Registry is being used to store the configuration information for the servers. It's a good location for this information because most servers are services, and services start running before a user even logs on.

- As Microsoft continues to aggressively promote the use of OLE technology, via such products as OLE databases and OLE transaction processing, the Registry will become increasingly important. This is because each OLE object extensively uses the Registry.

These developments make the Registry a popular and busy place.

This growing popularity of the Registry means developers must understand the Registry and have applications that talk to it. For example, if you write OLE code then you will have to be able to clean up the mess it makes.

Organization of the Book

As the title implies, this book is a guide to the vast amount of information stored within the Windows NT Registry. The Registry is a key component of the Windows NT operating system that stores and controls the access of information used to initialize and configure Windows NT applications. All technologies on the Windows NT platform also make extensive use of the Registry. The Windows NT Registry is the mechanism that allows applications to seamlessly integrate so many powerful technologies.

The *Windows NT Registry Guide* covers the information that enables the developers to see how this integration is possible through the use of the Windows NT Registry subkeys and name value pairs. Following is a more detailed description of each chapter in this book.

Chapter 1   In this chapter, we discuss what the Registry is used for and its database structure. We also define a key and describe how information is stored. Also discussed are the Registry's predecessors—their downfalls and why they were replaced. We further include a little about the files that make up the Registry and how all the pieces of the Registry interact. We end with instruction on how to back up the Registry and how to restore the backup.

Chapter 2   Chapter 2 is all about the Registry Editor, the only tool that Microsoft provides for editing the Registry. The Registry Editor is straightforward to use because it is much like the file editor Explorer. It is important for understanding the Registry because it gives a visual representation to the abstract database.

Chapter 3   Chapter 3 details the Registry APIs provided by Microsoft so that applications written in C++ can access the Registry. Because accessing the Registry is more important to applications than to users, the APIs are more robust than the Registry Editor. It is important to master the APIs before going on to Chapters 4 and 5.

Chapter 4   Chapter 4 focuses on how to use the Registry using the Win32 Registry API through the Visual Basic programming language. Visual Basic developers can learn how to properly use the Registry API, since how to do this isn't that straightforward from Visual Basic. After studying this chapter and its examples, a Visual Basic developer will have the knowledge needed to take advantage of the NT Registry.

Chapter 5   In Chapter 5, we cover how to write DLLs and executables that register themselves. We also include examples of two applications that use the Registry to interact with other applications: the Event Log and the Performance Monitor. We show you how to write to the Event Log and have your applications monitored by the Performance Monitor. More important, we discuss how they interact with other applications through the Registry. This type of interaction is a good example of Registry programming at its finest and should be used as a model for your applications.

Chapter 6   Chapter 6 describes the intricate role the Registry plays in supporting the ActiveX technology and its subtechnologies. The chapter covers the various identifier types and component categories contained within the Registry for use by ActiveX.

Chapter 7   Chapter 7 discusses programming extensions to the NT shell. You can extend the shell by writing handlers for various custom functions. The shell knows the handlers exist by reading the Registry. NT shell extension programming is a powerful tool. It also is an example of exposing COM (component object model) objects to an application through the Registry. In this case, the application is the shell and the handlers are COM objects. This is another great model on which to base your Registry work.

Chapter 1

Registry Structure

The Registry is laid out in a hierarchical structure of *keys* and *name-value pairs*. This structure is used as a central configuration database for the user, application, operating system, and computer information.

In this chapter, we discuss what the Registry is, what programs use the Registry for, and how the Registry structure is constructed. This practical information will form the basis for your understanding of the Registry. We also discuss the most important aspect of dealing with the Registry: backing it up.

The Registry's Hierarchical Structure

The hierarchical structure of the Registry resembles the directory structure of Windows. *Keys* can be thought of as folders and *name-value pairs* as files. The Registry Editor, Microsoft's main Registry manipulation tool, looks and feels like Explorer, the file and folder manipulation tool of Windows 95.

Keys

The hierarchical structure consists of keys—branches of the Registry tree. A **key** is a node of the hierarchical Registry structure. It consists of subkeys and name-value pairs. A **subkey** is the child of a parent key. A **name-value pair** is the holder of the data within the Registry. Each key may have any number of subkeys and/or name-value pairs. Each key has a name that must be unique to its parent. That name may be any combination of characters—lowercase, uppercase, numerals, and symbols—except for the backward slash (\). In this book, we use the backward slash as a delimiter to indicate a parent-subkey pairing, similar to how it is used in indicating subfolders of folders in the file directory structure; for example:

```
parent\subkey
```

HKEYs

An **HKEY** is a handle to the top-most keys of the Registry. HKEYs are defined in the Registry application program interface (API) and are the developer's access point to the rest of the tree. There are two major keys: HKEY_LOCAL_MACHINE and HKEY_USERS. There also are four minor keys derived from the major keys, as follows:

- HKEY_CLASSES_ROOT

  HKEY_CLASSES_ROOT derives from HKEY_LOCAL_MACHINE\ SOFTWARE\Classes. It provides backward compatibility with the Windows 3.1 Registration Information Editor. It also can be used as a shortcut to easily reference HKEY_LOCAL_MACHINE\SOFTWARE\ Classes.

- HKEY_CURRENT_USER

  HKEY_CURRENT_USER derives from HKEY_USERS\<subkey>, where <subkey> is the current user. This HKEY is set when a user logs on to the operating system. Applications looking for current data on the logged-on user need to look only in this minor key.

- HKEY_CURRENT_CONFIG

  HKEY_CURRENT_CONFIG derives from HKEY_LOCAL_MACHINE\ Config\<subkey> in Windows 95, where <subkey> is the numbered hardware configuration currently being used. The root key is present only in Windows 95. Some Windows 95 machines might have two hardware configurations; for example, laptops have one configuration for docked and one for undocked.

■ HKEY_DYN_DATA

HKEY_DYN_DATA is a dynamic key. It is created anew each time the operating system is started. All the information under HKEY_DYN_DATA is stored in RAM.

Name-Value Pairs

A name-value pair has three parts: the name of the value, the value itself, and the data type, that is, the type of value. A name-value pair is commonly called a *value.* However, in this book we use *name-value pair* because that term is more accurate and less confusing than *value*, which can have other meanings. A name-value pair is the component in the Registry that stores the actual data. Using the key path as the locator and the name as the reference, you can extract the value from the name-value pair.

Data Types

The value of a name-value pair may be one of many data types. The three main types are DWORD, string, and binary. The other lesser-used ones are DWORD in big endian format, expanded string, Unicode symbolic link, device-driver resource list, and array of strings. There also is an undefined type.

The DWORD data type stores DWORDs. A **DWORD** is a number that is represented by double words, or 4 bytes. It cannot be negative. It is the only way to store numbers in the Registry. There are no C equivalents to int, long, or short.

A **string** data type is just that—a string. It is useful for writing strings to the Registry, since users can read and alter them easily. Most strings are either names of applications or paths to files.

The **binary** data type stores data in binary format. This is the "everything else" data type. That is, if you can't write it as a string or a number, then write it in binary to the Registry. The only problem with doing this is that you also have to read it in binary.

The other data types have very specific uses. We don't discuss them in this book. We recommend that you try to stay with the three main data types when programming in the Registry.

What the Registry Is Used For

The Registry stores information about the following:

- State information about applications and the operating system

- The current user and other users of the system (in a sense, the "state" of the user)

- Configuration information for services and other applications that don't have a GUI (graphical user interface)

- Configuration information of the operating system

We discuss state shortly. First, we give a little background about Windows applications that will help make understanding state easier.

Applications in the Windows operating system usually consist of compiled binary files called *executables* and their supporting components called *DLLs*. Once compiled, executables and DLLs cannot be changed. When either executables or DLLs are run or open, they load into the computer's RAM. Each running application consists of an executable section and a data section. The executable section of the program never changes, but the data section does, depending on the content of the executable section. For example, say you open Notepad (notepad.exe) and type "Hello". The data section of memory would contain "Hello". Then you close the application. The next time you open it, you type "Goodbye"; the data section of memory would then contain "Goodbye". Generally, when you close an application the data section of memory is lost, but the executable section stays around in the executable file on the computer's hard disk.

State

State is that part of an application's configuration that can be changed. For example, suppose you open Notepad and change the font of the type from Times Roman to Helvetica. You have changed Notepad's state. If you then close Notepad, the Registry will save the previous state so that the next time Notepad opens, the state will be how you left it. Reopen Notepad, and the application will read the Registry and figure out the type's font—in this case, Helvetica.

The font state data is stored in the Registry at the key HKEY_LOCAL_MACHINE\Software\Microsoft\Notepad. Each software company has its own key located under HKEY_LOCAL_MACHINE\Software. For example, Microsoft's key is HKEY_LOCAL_MACHINE\Software\Microsoft.

In addition, each application has a key under the name of the software company that developh it, as illustrated by the previous Notepad example.

Operating System Configuration

The operating system is configured using the Registry, and its state and configuration are stored there. When the computer is shut down, the Registry is saved on the hard drive. When the computer is turned on, the operating system loads the Registry and reads the saved configuration information in order to restore the operating system's saved state. The information that is saved includes the path and directory information, like this:

HKEY_LOCAL_MACHINE\SOFTWARE\Microsoft\Windows\
CurrentVersion

Notice that the operating system information is included in the same key under which applications are located—HKEY_LOCAL_MACHINE. This is because the operating system can be considered an application, in the sense of its stored state information, that is.

Also, note that certain configurations of the operating system are not saved in HKEY_LOCAL_MACHINE\SOFTWARE\Microsoft\Windows or any of its subkeys. This includes the background color and icon arrangement, which is part of the user's state, since the settings of these features are configured differently for each user of the operating system.

User's State

Each user has a saved state in the Registry. That state contains settings for screen color, loaded applications, and other preferences that the user has configured for the Desktop. It is used by the Desktop when the user logs on. At the same time, the HKEY_CURRENT_USER is assigned to a subkey of HKEY_USERS based on the log-on name.

Services

All services and some other types of executables do not have a GUI, so the configuration of these executables is usually handled through the Registry. The Registry has a section set aside for services:

HKEY_LOCAL_MACHINE\SYSTEM\CurrentControlSet\Services

Services are executables that Windows NT runs in the background. They are usually loaded when the operating system starts. Examples of services are the Internet Information Server, the SQL Server, and the Windows NT file server. Each service handles configuration differently. The Internet Information Server allows you to change some parameters through its Internet Service Manager GUI, but others can be changed only through the Registry. The SQL Server handles all its configuration management through its Enterprise Manager GUI application.

Before the Registry

Before the Registry was developed, software depended on other means to store state and configuration data: the proprietary state file or the .ini file.

Proprietary State Files

During the early days of application software development, each application had its own proprietary state file in which it stored state information. When the application loaded, it would load the state file and read the state information. When the application closed, it would write the state information to the file. Usually, the files were in binary format. This made them hard to read and debug.

However, software companies, including Microsoft, soon found this type of implementation to be inefficient. Every time state information needed to be saved, software companies had to reimplement the loading and unloading process of the state information. This wasted resources. More important, product support personnel had no way to view or change the state information of a particular application or of the operating system because all the state information was in binary format.

.ini Files

.ini files were the second wave of development of state files. They were designed to fix the problems with proprietary state files. Each application could have one or many .ini files. As with proprietary state files, when the application loaded, the application would read the .ini file and use the information therein to return the application to its previous state. When the application closed, it would write the state information to the .ini file for saving. The operating system also had .ini files that defined its state and configuration. The two main operating system .ini files were system.ini and win.ini.

.ini files had several advantages. First, they were in a standard text format that could be used by everyone. For example, product support personnel could read and edit them. Also, an API was written in order to access them; hence, the reloading and unloading of information was handled in common reusable code.

However, .ini files also had their problems. First, they were designed to be either in the application's directory or in the system's path. The notion of an application's relying on paths went out of favor because of problems with path manipulation and path length. Paths were hard to manipulate because in early operating systems, such as Windows 3.1, the paths where written in string format in the autoexec.bat file. This format was hard to work with and for many users had to be adjusted later, after installation. Also, in Windows 3.1 the path was limited to 256 characters— too short for a machine that was running many applications.

Second, .ini files were hard for installation applications to locate. This was because a user could install the application anywhere on the hard drive; hence, the .ini file likewise could be anywhere on the drive. Third, .ini files could not be larger than 64K. The size limitation became an issue particularly with the system.ini and win.ini files. These files could grow quite large depending on the number of applications installed. Accessing .ini files, especially large ones, was slow, since Windows performed a linear search for the searched item on the file. Fourth, .ini files were hard to administer and secure over a network. And finally, the data in an .ini file was untyped. This meant that programmers had to cast numbers to strings. Doing this introduced errors into code, especially when users modified numbers with a text editor.

The Registry addressed many of these problems. Its central location fixed problems application developers had locating .ini files along paths. Also, the Registry has unlimited capacity, thus the 64K size restriction of some .ini files is eliminated. As an index database, the Registry is quicker to search. Finally, it allows many data types, so it forces data to adhere to a specific type. This allows application developers to query the data with confidence. For example, with .ini files, data came back only as strings. If the data was supposed to be a number, it would have to be converted from a string to a number. However, because the Registry can be queried for either a number or a string, developers can easily retrieve the information they want.

Although the Registry solved the .ini file problems, it wasn't immediately embraced because implementing the .ini files into the Registry requires more work than most software companies want to do. As a result, many .ini files—system.ini and win.ini, for example—remain in Windows NT 4.0 and Windows 95, in particular because 16-bit software needs them.

The Registration Information Editor

Windows 3.1 included a registration database called the Registration Information Editor (RIE) that handled file extensions. This database could be considered the early predecessor of the current Registry. Both are accessed via regedit.exe. However, the RIE was stored in only one file—reg.dat—whereas the Registry is stored in multiple files. Also, the RIE lacked the functionality that the current Registry Editor contains.

The Registry's File Structure

The Registry combines the text .ini files into proprietary binary files. Now, going from readable text files to proprietary binary files might seem like a step backward. However, Microsoft has provided developers with an API to access the Registry and all users with an editor to edit the Registry, so editing the binary files is easier that it used to be.

Windows 95 has more Registry files than does Windows NT 4.0. In the former, the Registry files are user.dat and system.dat and are hidden files in the c:\windows directory. (In this book, we assume Windows is on the c: drive. You should reference whatever drive is storing the reference files.) The user.dat file contains all the information in HKEY_USERS. The system.dat file contains all the information in HKEY_LOCAL_MACHINE.

In Windows NT, the Registry files are stored in "hives" in c:\system32\config. A **hive** is a binary-formatted Registry file that contains a subkey of a major HKEY. Hives do not have extensions; however, they do have names. Table 1.1 lists the hives—their names and their associated subkeys.

Table 1.1 Hives

Hive Name	Associated Subkey
system	HKEY_LOCAL_MACHINE\SYSTEM
software	HKEY_LOCAL_MACHINE\SOFTWARE
security	HKEY_LOCAL_MACHINE\SECURITY
sam	HKEY_LOCAL_MACHINE\SAM
default	HKEY_USERS\.DEFAULT
userdiff	HKEY_USERS\<All Others>

In Chapter 3, we discuss how to save a hive using the Registry API and how to restore a hive to the Registry.

Safeguarding Your Registry

This book is all about the Registry. But it is not about how to destroy your operating system and having to reinstall everything! Messing with the state or configuration information of the Registry could cause you to lose it all. So in this section, we show you how to back up your Registry, *before* you begin tinkering with it.

Note: Having given this good advice, one of the authors (Wayne Berry) did not take it. When preparing some of the examples for later chapters, he destroyed the Registry and had to reinstall it. So be warned: It could happen to anyone.

Backing Up

Remember that the Registry is dynamic. So each time you begin to mess with it, first back up the old files. By doing this, you will always have a copy of the latest Registry.

Backing Up in Windows 95

To back up the Windows 95 Registry, follow these steps:

1. Create a directory under c:\windows\system32 called backup.

2. Copy system.dat and user.dat to the new directory, c:\windows\system32\backup.

Backing Up in Windows NT 4.0

Don't even bother backing up Windows NT if your operating system is installed on an NTFS drive. Why? Because if the operating system doesn't come up due to a problem with the Registry, then you cannot read the NTFS drive. No operating system, no NTFS drive. And if you can't reach the drive, then you can't restore the Registry files. We recommend that you always install the operating system on a FAT drive.

To back up the Windows NT Registry, follow these steps:

1. Create a directory under c:\winnt\system32\config called backup.

2. Copy all the files *without extensions* to the new directory, c:\winnt\system32\config\backup.

Now you're set. If you have any problems with the Registry, you can restore it from your backup.

Restoring the Registry

Here's how to restore your backups, should you ever need to do so. Regardless of whether you're in Windows 95 or Windows NT, the first step is to boot to DOS. In this way, you can avoid the crashed operating system. Then move to the instructions that follow, depending on your operating system.

Restoring in Windows 95

1. Copy the system.dat and user.dat from the backup directory c:\windows\system32\backup to the directory c:\windows\system32.

2. Reboot to Windows 95. The operating system might contain characteristics of the system state that existed when you last backed up the files, but at least you don't have to reinstall the operating system and all your applications.

Restoring in Windows NT 4.0

1. Copy all the files *with no extensions* from the backup directory c:\winnt\system32\config\backup to the directory c:\winnt\system32\config.

2 Reboot to Windows NT 4.0. The operating system might contain characteristics of the system state that existed when you backed up the files, but at least you don't have to reinstall the operating system and all the applications.

You Didn't Back Up!

Say you didn't take our advice. You didn't back up your Registry. You now are frantically looking for a solution to get your operating system working again. What can you do?

You can try to restore your operating system by using the following desperate techniques.

Salvaging Windows 95

1. Back up the nonworking files by copying all the files in the directory c:\windows\system into a new directory called c:\winnt\system\backup.

2. Copy the user.dao file over the user.dat file and the system.dao file over the system.dat file.

3. Reboot the operating system.

Salvaging Windows NT 4.0

1. Back up the nonworking files by copying all the files in the directory c:\winnt\system32\config into a new directory called c:\winnt\system32\config\backup.

2. Copy each *.alt file that is in c:\winnt\system32\config over the file in the same directory with the same name that does not have an extension. These are Registry files that are one reboot old. For example:

```
C: Cd \winnt\system32\config
Copy *.alt *.
```

3. Reboot the operating system.

Note: Because the operating system and other applications need information in the Registry in order to boot properly, we recommend you back up your Registry before going on to the next chapter.

Chapter 2

The Registry Editor

The primary tool for viewing and editing the Registry is the Registry Editor. The Registry Editor shows the Registry in a tree view. This tree view is how most people visualize the Registry, even though the Registry has no real "look," since it is an invisible database that can be depicted only by a GUI.

Sorting Out Versions of the Editor

Several versions of the Registry Editor were released with different versions of Windows. Of these, some have the same GUI, including the one that comes with Windows NT 4.0 and Windows 95. Others share the same executable name across different versions of Windows but have different GUIs. (See Table 2.1.) Having all these variations sometimes causes confusion, so we want to clarify what is going on before we talk about how the GUIs work.

The Registry Editor that shipped with Windows NT 3.5 and Windows NT 3.51 (as well as with Windows 3.1 and Windows for Work Groups) was hard to use and very limited in scope. The newer one that ships with Windows NT 3.51, Windows NT 4.0, and Windows 95 is much improved. Right away you can tell the new GUI from the old because it looks and feels a lot like the Windows NT 4.0 and Windows 95 Explorer. For example, each HKEY branches out of a root of My Computer in the left-hand view of the tree and name-value pairs for the selected key appear in the right-hand view of the tree. If you had to work with the old Registry Editor, you'll really like the new one.

In this book, we discuss how to use the newer version, but you need to be aware that the older one exists.

Table 2.1 Registry editors in Windows releases

Operating System	Executable Name	Version Number	GUI Type
Windows NT 4.0	regedit.exe	4.00	New GUI Version
Windows 95	regedit.exe	4.00.950	New GUI Version
Windows NT 3.51	regedit.exe	3.10	Old GUI Version
Windows NT 3.51	regedt32.exe	3.51	New GUI Version

Notice that Windows NT 3.51 has two versions of the Registry Editor. One was released with Windows NT 3.50, and the other, with a newer-style GUI, was released with Windows NT 3.51.

Starting the Registry Editor

The Registry Editor is not a toy. With a couple of mouse clicks in the Editor, a user can easily destroy the operating system. Hence, the Registry Editor is not available on the Start menu in either Windows NT 4.0 or Windows 95. And you won't find it in any of the groups under Windows NT 3.51.

To start the Registry Editor under Windows NT 4.0 and Windows 95, follow these steps. See also Figure 2.1.

1. Click Start | Run.

2. Type the name of the Registry Editor's executable: regedit.exe.

3. Click OK.

And under Windows NT 3.51:

1. Hold down the Control key and press Escape.

2. In the cmd edit box, type the name of the Registry Editor's executable: regedt32.exe.

3. Click Run.

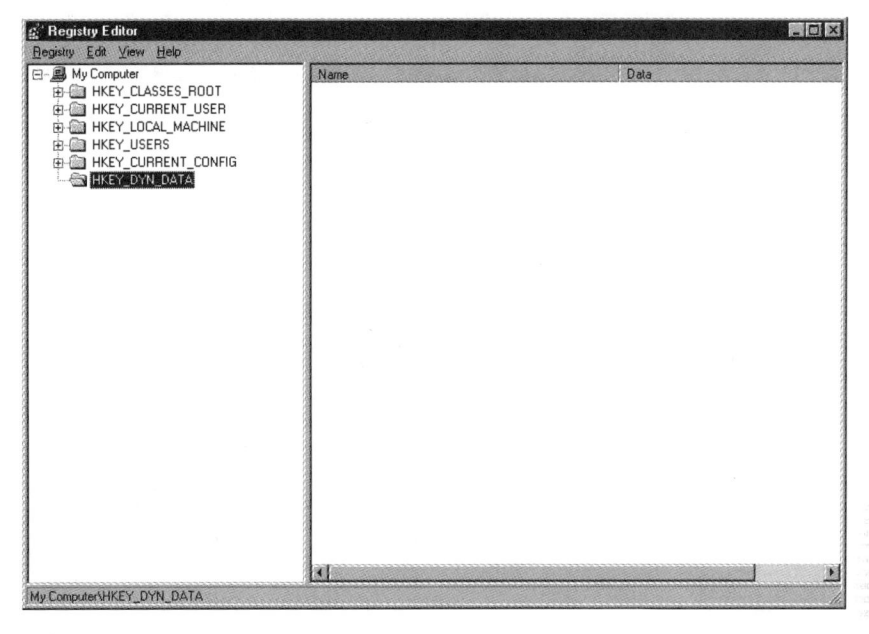

Figure 2.1 The new Registry Editor

Expanding a Key

You can expand a key in several ways:

- Double-click the key's folder.

- Click the plus symbol next to the key's folder.

- Highlight the key you want to expand in the left-hand tree view of the Registry Editor. Then right-click the highlighted key and select Expand from the drop-down menu.

Figure 2.2 shows the key HKEY_LOCAL_MACHINE in Windows NT 4.0 opened to expose its subkeys HARDWARE, SAM, SECURITY, SOFTWARE, and SYSTEM. Notice that there is no plus box next to the SECURITY folder. A plus indicates a folder can be expanded; no plus means the folder cannot be expanded.

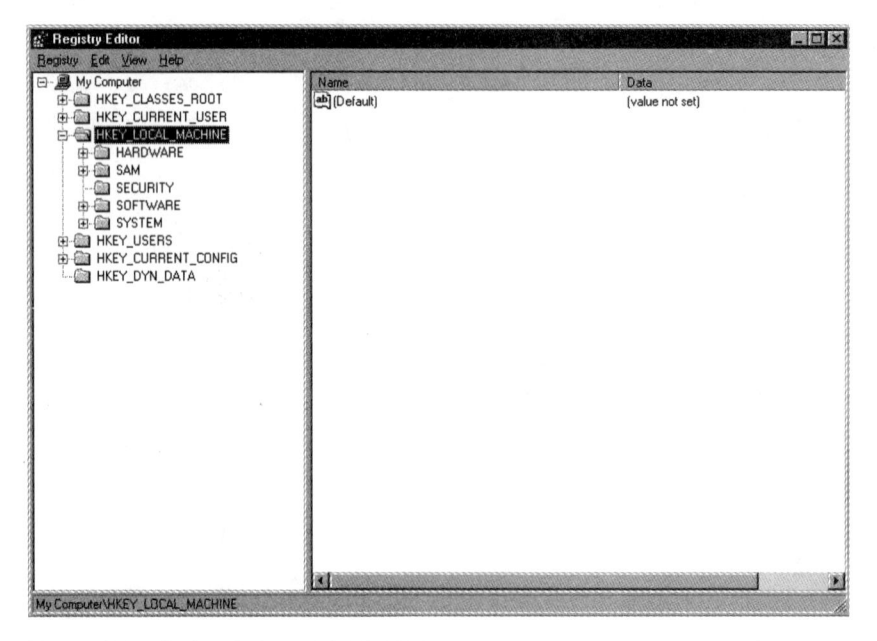

Figure 2.2 HKEY_LOCAL _MACHINE expanded in Windows NT 4.0

Viewing Name-Value Pairs in a Key

To view the name-value pairs in a key, click the key's folder to open it. The pairs will display in the right-hand view. For example, click the folder of key HKEY_LOCAL_MACHINE. Then click the folder of its subkey HARDWARE. Next, click HARDWARE's subkey, DESCRIPTION, followed by DESCRIPTION's subkey, System. The name-value pairs will display in the right-hand view of the Registry Editor. Figure 2.3 shows the result on our machine. You likely won't have the same values for the pairs, but they should be similar.

Notice in the right-hand view the graphic with a red "ab" to the immediate left of the names Identifier, SystemBiosDate, and VideoBiosDate. This graphic is a type identifier that indicates that the values of those name-value pairs are of type string. The graphic type identifier that contains blue zeros and ones indicates that the values of Configuration Data, SystemBiosVersion, and VideoBiosVersion are of type binary.

Every key has a default value. In Figure 2.3, the default value has not been set. The default value can be only of type REG_SZ.

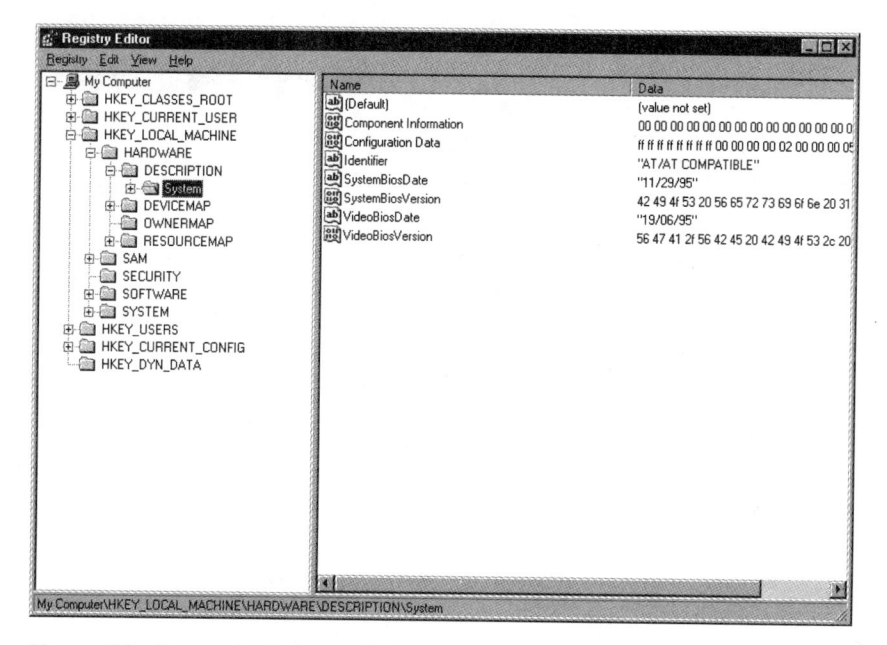

Figure 2.3 Expanded view of HKEY_LOCAL_MACHINE\HARDWARE\
Description\System in Windows NT 4.0

Creating a Key

Changing values in the Registry can be very dangerous, since the
operating system and other applications rely on the Registry in order to
operate properly. So before you begin to work with the Registry Editor,
you need to make a test key in the Registry that you can use for examples
without effecting other components.

To create a test key to use for examples, follow these steps:

1. Click the plus sign next to HKEY_LOCAL_MACHINE and then click
   SOFTWARE to open the subkey HKEY_LOCAL_MACHINE | SOFT-
   WARE. For illustration purposes, we'll add a new subkey to SOFTWARE.
   A drop-down menu appears.

2. Select New from the drop-down. A second drop-down menu appears.
   Figure 2.4 shows the result.

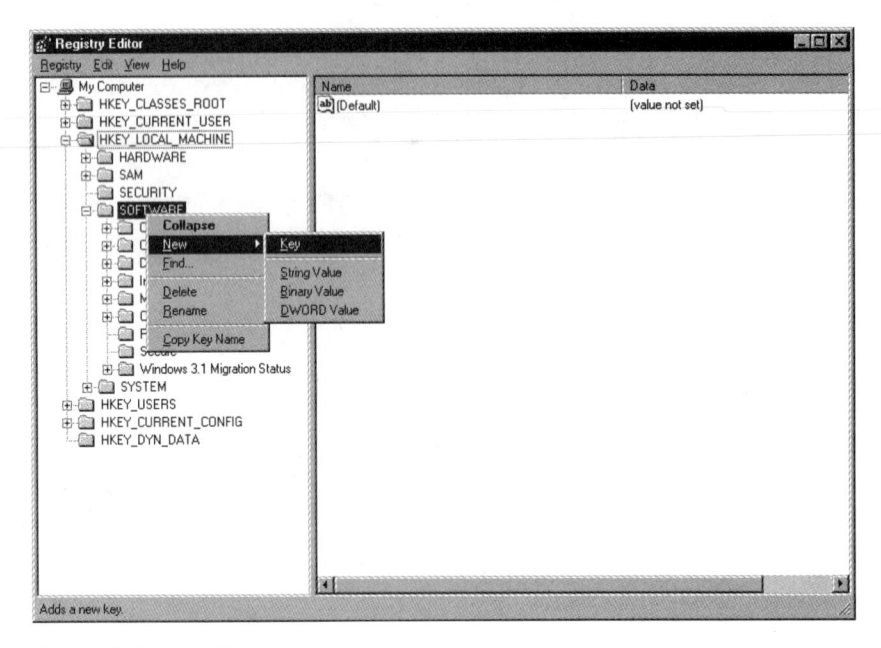

Figure 2.4 Creating a key

3. Select Key from the second drop-down. A new key appears in the tree as a subkey of SOFTWARE. Initially the new key has the name of New Key #1, which is highlighted, as shown in Figure 2.5.

4. Rename the key by typing its new name, in this case, WidgetWare.

5. Press Enter to cause the name change to take effect.

You can create a key also by using the Menu Bar, as follows:

1. Highlight the parent key in the left-hand tree view of the Registry Editor.

2. Click Edit | New | Key. A new key appears in the tree as a subkey of SOFTWARE with the initial name of New Key #1, which is highlighted, as shown in Figure 2.5.

3. Rename the key as described in the previous steps 4 and 5.

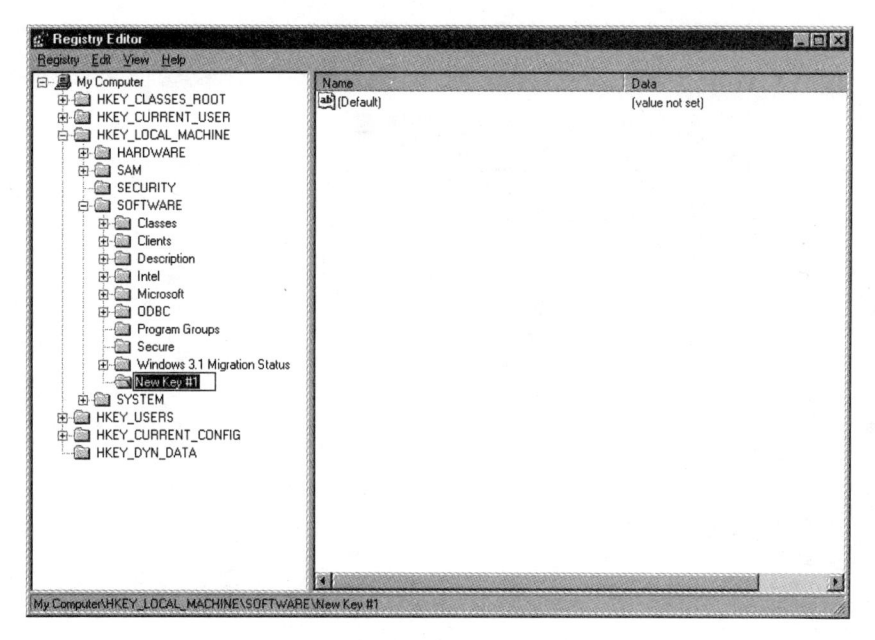

Figure 2.5 The new key in the Registry

Changing the Default Value

In the last section, we created the key WidgetWare. Next, we'll change its default value. To change the default value, follow these steps. See also Figure 2.6.

1. In the right-hand view, double-click the key name of the name-value pair shown, in this case, Default. The Edit String dialog box appears. This dialog box consists of two parts. One holds the name of the name-value pair, and the other holds the value of the pair.

2. Type the new value in the "Value data" field.

3. Click OK.

Caution: There's a bug in the release version of NT 4.0 that affects the editing of a key's default value. If no value is associated with the default name-value pair, then the Edit String dialog box inserts in the "Value data" field the last string edited by the Registry Editor before you opened the dialog box. You must type in the correct value before closing the dialog box or the

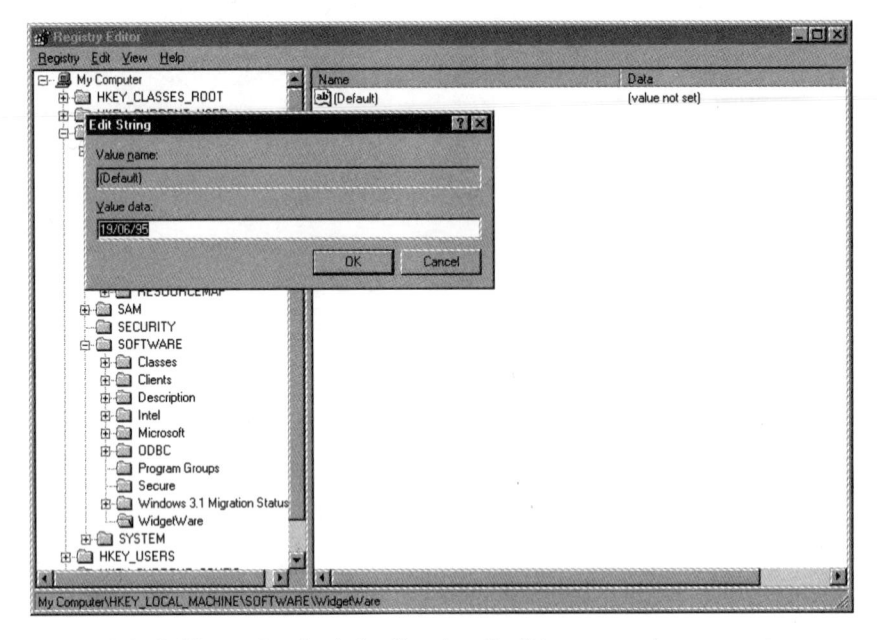

Figure 2.6 Editing a key's default value. In this case, a buggy value was inserted as a value.

wrong value will be entered. Figure 2.6 illustrates how this happens. The right-hand view confirms that there is no value. The last string edited happened to be 19/06/95, so that value was automatically entered in the "Value data" field. You would need to type the correct value before clicking OK.

Adding a Name-Value Pair to a Key

To add a name-value to a key, follows these steps:

1. In the left-hand tree view, click the name of the key to which you want to add a name-value pair.

2. Move the mouse over the right-hand view and right-click. A drop-down menu appears containing one selection, New.

3. Click New. A second drop-down menu appears. See Figure 2.7.

4. From the second drop-down, select either String Value, Binary Value, or DWORD Value. If you choose DWORD Value, a new name-value

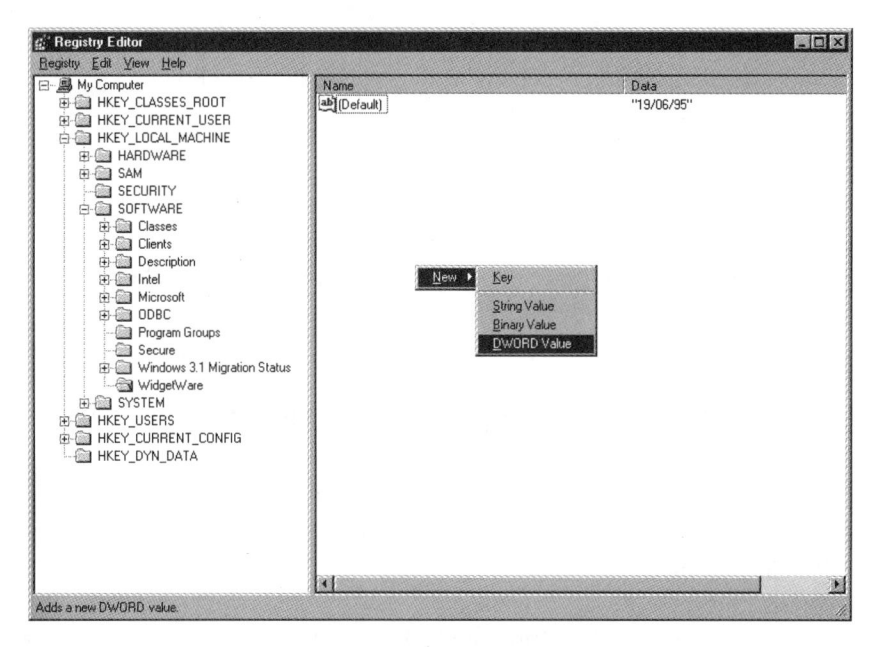

Figure 2.7 Adding a name-value pair to a key

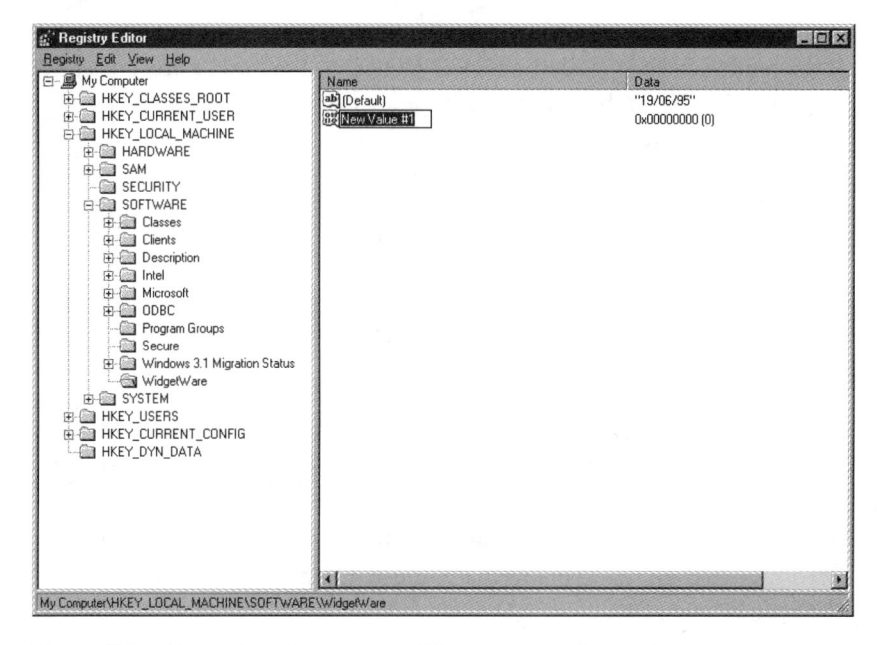

Figure 2.8 Changing the name of the name-value pair

pair appears in the right-hand view with the name section highlighted and the default name of New Value #1. See Figure 2.8.

5. Type a new name in the name part of the name-value pair; for example, WidgetCount.

Note: Of all the data types that the Registry uses, only the string, binary, and DWORD types can be created with the Registry Editor. The others can be created only by using the API.

Changing the Value of a Name-Value Pair

Now that we've created the WidgetCount name-value pair, we'll next change its value. Doing this is a lot like changing the value of the default name-value pair. Follow these steps:

1. In the right-hand view, double-click the key name of the name-value pair shown. A dialog box appears.

   The type of box depends on the type of value. Because the value in this example is a DWORD, the Edit DWORD Value dialog box appears. See Figure 2.9. If you had double-clicked a string value instead, the Edit String dialog box would have appeared, as it did when we changed the default value earlier in the chapter. The same is true with a binary value. Double-clicking the value brings up the Edit Binary Value dialog box.

   The dialog box consist of two parts. One holds the name of the name-value pair, and the other holds the value of the pair.

2. Type the new value in the "Value data" field. In the case of a DWORD, you can edit the value in either base ten or base sixteen. In the Base group, edit in base ten by clicking the "Decimal" radio button and edit in base sixteen by clicking the "Hexadecimal" radio button. For our example, we change the value of WidgetCount to 10. Note that you cannot change the name of the name-value pair in the Edit DWORD Value dialog box.

3. Click OK. WidgetCount's value is displayed in the right-hand view in both decimal and hexadecimal forms.

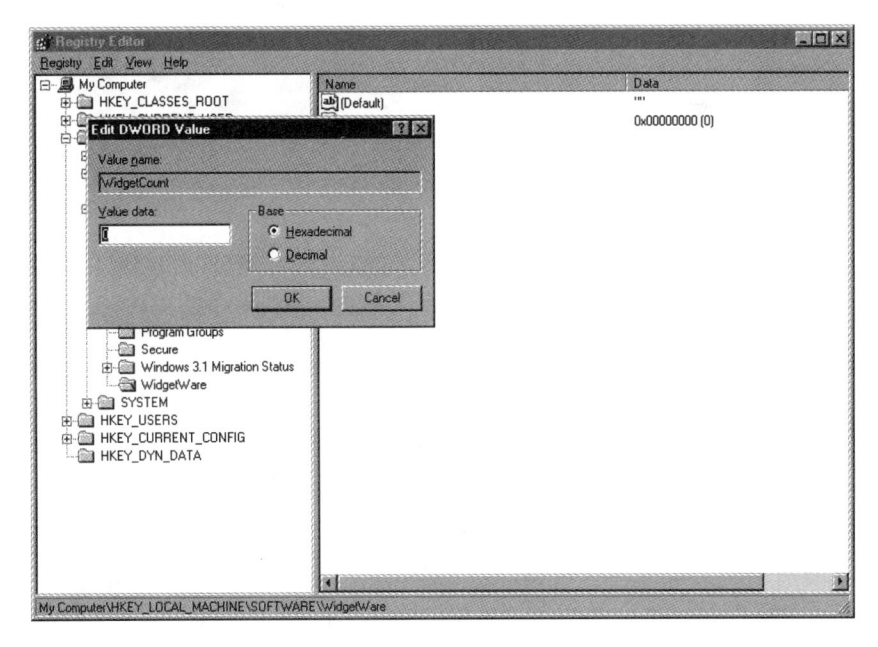

Figure 2.9 Changing the value of a DWORD using the Edit DWORD Value dialog box

When the value is a string, double-clicking the value's name in the right-hand view brings up the Edit String dialog box. Both the name and the value display in the dialog box, but only the value can be edited. For example, change the value to Widget. See Figure 2.10.

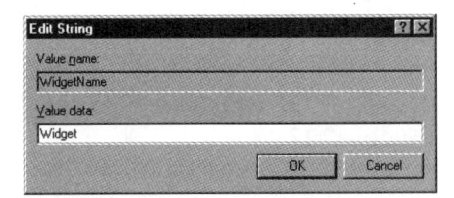

Figure 2.10 Changing the value of a string using the Edit String dialog box

When the value is a binary, double-clicking the value's name in the right-hand view brings up the Edit Binary Value dialog box. Both the name and the value display in the dialog, but only the value can be edited. You can edit the data in either hexadecimal or ANSI. For example, change the value to Widget. See Figure 2.11.

23

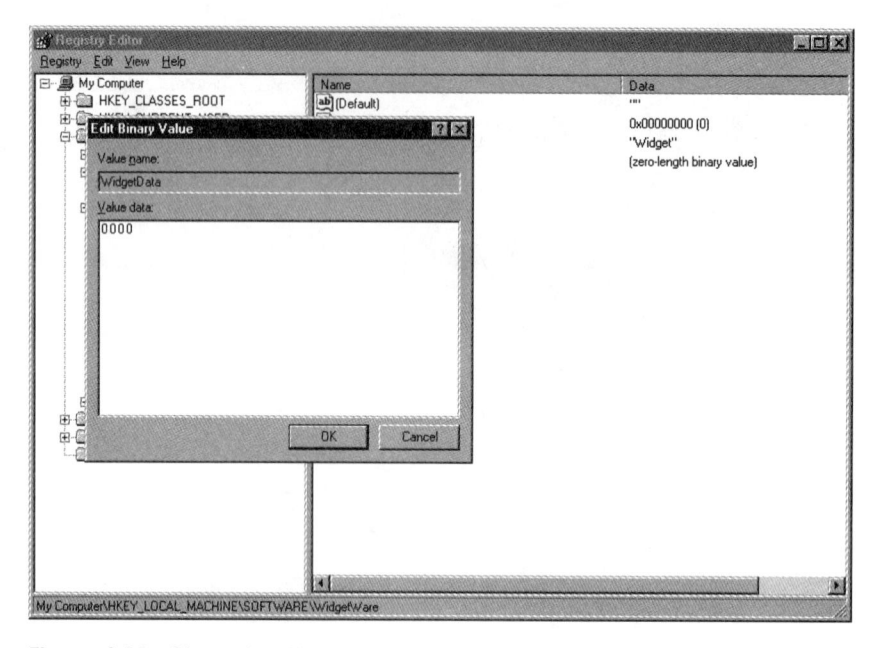

Figure 2.11 Changing the value of a binary using the Edit Binary Value dialog box

Renaming Keys and Name-Value Pairs

To rename a Registry key, follow these steps:

1. In the left-hand tree view, click to highlight the name of the key whose name you want to change.

2. With the name highlighted, right-click the mouse over the selected key. A drop-down menu appears. See Figure 2.12.

3. Click Rename from the drop-down menu. The key name appears in the tree view in edit mode (the text cursor is within the highlighted name).

4. Type the new name and press Return. For example, change WidgetWare to Widget Software in Figure 2.12.

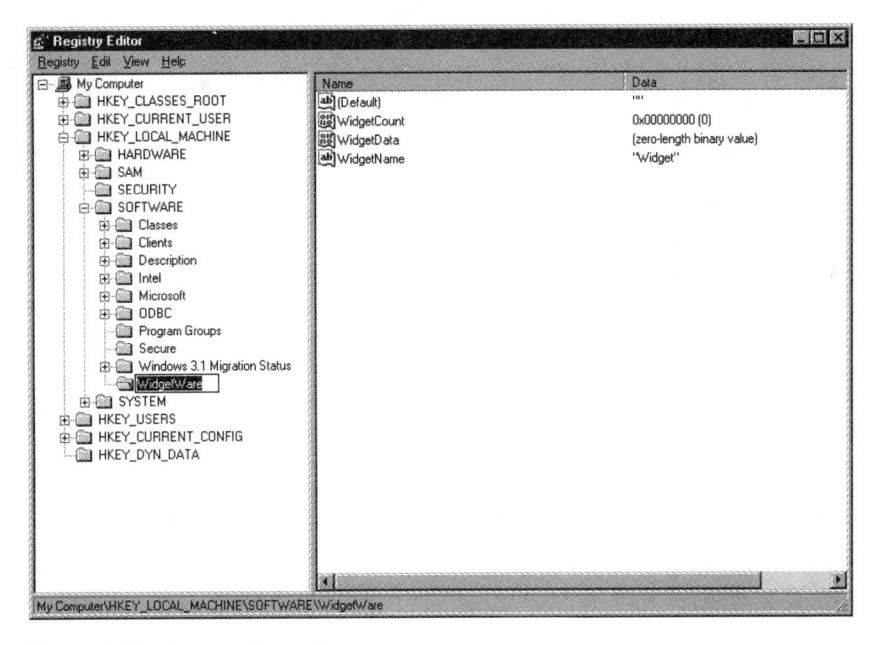

Figure 2.12 Renaming a key

Renaming a name-value pair is a lot like renaming a key. Follow these steps:

1. In the right-hand tree view, click to highlight the name-value pair whose name you want to change.

2. With the name highlighted, right-click the mouse over the selected key. A drop-down menu appears.

3. Click Rename from the drop-down. The key name appears in the tree view in edit mode.

4. Type in the new name and press Return. For example, change the name WidgetCount to WidgetDateLength. See Figure 2.13.

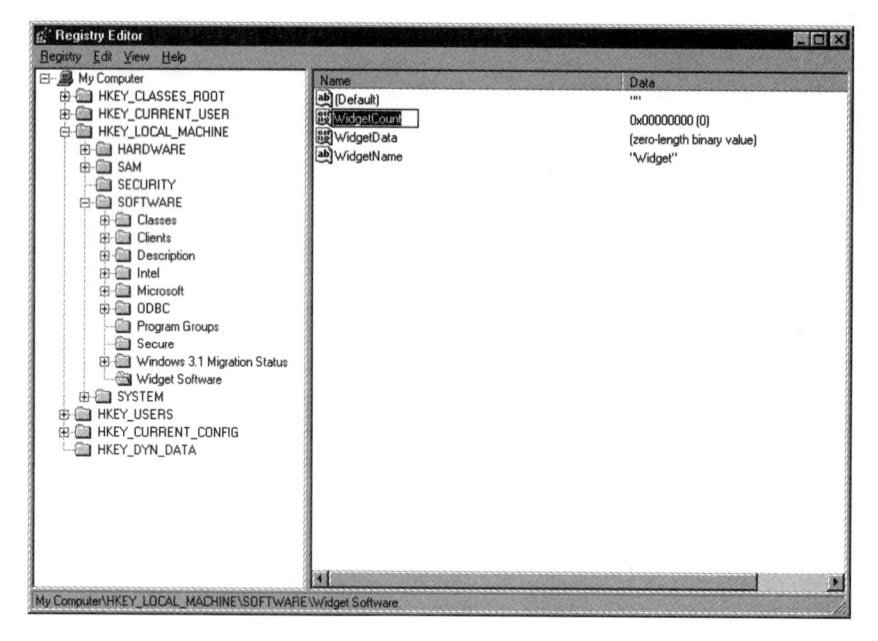

Figure 2.13 Renaming a name-value pair

Deleting a Key or a Name-Value Pair

Warning: Deleting a key or name-value pair is a permanent action. It cannot be undone.

To delete a key, follow these steps:

1. In the left-hand tree view, click to highlight the key whose name you want to delete; for example, the key WidgetSoftware.

2. With the name highlighted, right-click the mouse over the selected key. A drop-down menu appears. See Figure 2.14.

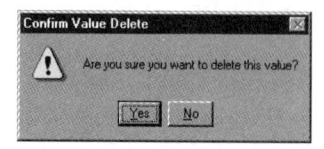

Figure 2.14 Deleting a key

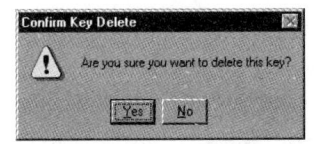

Figure 2.15 Confirming the deletion of a key

3. Click Delete from the drop-down. The Confirm Key Delete dialog box appears.

4. Click OK to permanently delete the key. See Figure 2.15.

Note: You cannot delete the root keys:

- HKEY_LOCAL_MACHINE

- HKEY_CLASSES_ROOT

- HKEY_CURRENT_USER

- HKEY_USER

- HKEY_CURRENT_CONFIG

- HKEY_DYN_DATA

To delete a name-value pair:

1. In the right-hand tree view, click to highlight the name-value pair that you want to delete; for example, the name-value pair WidgetData.

2. With the name highlighted, right-click the mouse over the selected key. A drop-down menu appears.

3. Click Delete from the drop-down. The Confirm Value Delete dialog box appears.

4. Click OK to permanently delete the name-value pair.

Note: You cannot delete the default name-value pair. Following the previous procedure to delete the default name-value pair will not delete the value but will return the value to "value not set."

Copying the Key Path

Sometimes key paths are very long, so copying a path can be very useful. Paths are copied to the Clipboard. To copy the key path to the Clipboard, follow these steps:

1. In the left-hand tree view, click the key to which you want to refer.

2. From the Menu Bar, click Edit | Copy Key Name.

To view the key path, open Notepad as follows:

1. Select Start | Run.

2. In the "Open" field, type Notepad. Notepad opens with a blank page.

3. From Notepad's Menu Bar, click Edit | Paste. The path to the key you selected displays.

You can use this technique to paste key paths, for example, into email or text for a book.

Finding Keys, Values, and/or Data

The Registry is very big. Sometimes a manual search won't yield what you're looking for. The Registry Editor's Find utility can help you find things fast.

To find a key, a value, and/or some data with the Registry Editor, follow these steps. See also Figure 2.16.

1. In the left-hand tree view, click to highlight the name of the key you want to search. The Find utility that comes with the Registry Editor will search all the subkeys of the highlighted key for the requested key, value, or data.

2. Right-click the highlighted key. A drop-down menu appears.

3. Click Find... from that drop-down menu. The Find dialog box appears.

4. Type in the "Find what" field the item you are looking for.

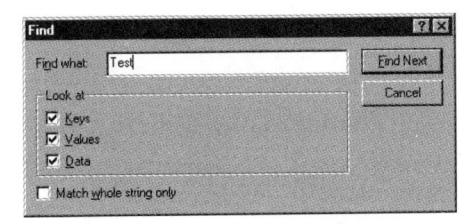

Figure 2.16 Finding keys, values, and data

5. Choose from the "Look at" check box list where you want to search: Keys, Values, or Data or any combination of the three.

6. Click Find Next. The Registry Editor begins to search the Registry.

The first occurrence of what you are looking for will be opened in the Registry Editor for you. To find the next occurrence, press F3 or go to the Menu Bar and select Edit | Find Next.

You also can search by simply choosing Edit | Find from the Menu Bar. Doing this will take you to the Find… dialog box. The steps are the same from there.

Connecting and Disconnecting to and from Another Registry

You can use the Registry Editor to edit the Registry of another computer. However, you first must meet these requirements:

■ Your computer must have a network connection to the computer to which you want to connect.

■ You must be an administrator on the computer to which you want to connect.

Connecting to Another Computer

To connect to the Registry of another computer, follow these steps:

1. Click Registry | Connect Network Registry… . The Connect Network Registry dialog box appears.

2. Type the name of the computer to which you want to connect. For example, Dartdrop.

3. Click OK. The name of the computer to which you have connected appears in the left-hand tree view of the Registry Editor as a separate root. It should sit below My Computer in the Registry. See Figure 2.17.

Figure 2.17 Connecting to another computer's Registry; in this case, the computer is Dartdrop

Disconnecting from Another Registry

To disconnect from the Registry of another computer, follow these steps:

1. In the left-hand tree view of the Registry Editor, click to highlight the name of the computer from which you want to disconnect.

2. With the name highlighted, right-click the mouse over the selected computer's name. A drop-down menu appears.

3. From that drop-down menu, select Disconnect. See Figure 2.18.

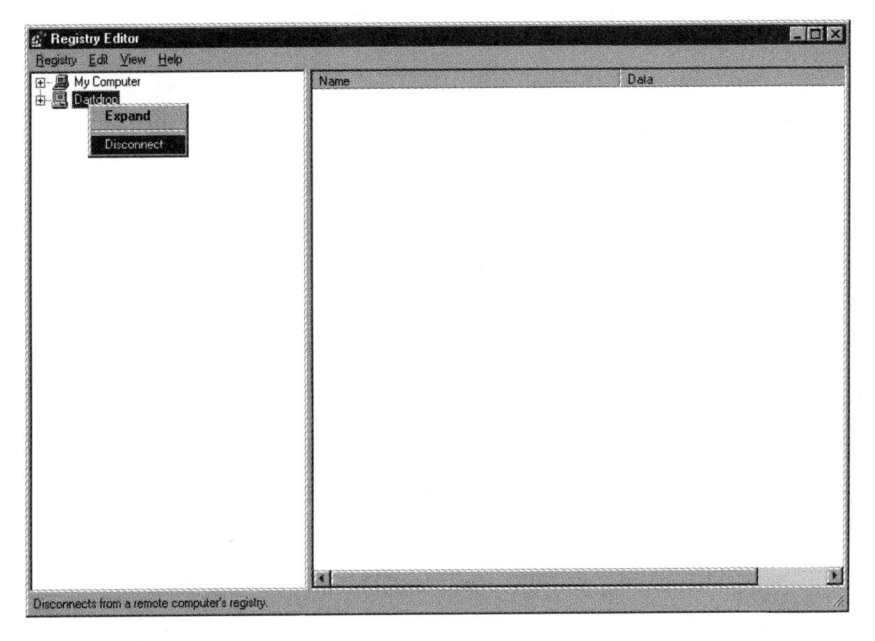

Figure 2.18 Disconnecting from another computer's Registry

You also can disconnect by highlighting the computer name as described in step one and then clicking Registry | Disconnect from the Menu Bar. The drop-down menu will appear as before. The steps are the same from there.

Exporting All or Part of a Registry File

One of the most important and interesting actions you can do with the Registry Editor is to export all or part (a branch) of the Registry as a text file. The exported text file contains a scripting language that the Registry Editor can read in order to create Registry keys. The power of the scripting language lies in the fact that you can edit it by hand in order to change the Registry. We discuss the scripting language in detail later in the chapter. Now we take a look at the feature of the Registry Editor that creates the scripts based on the current Registry: exporting the Registry file.

To export a branch of the Registry file, follow these steps. (See Figure 2.19.)

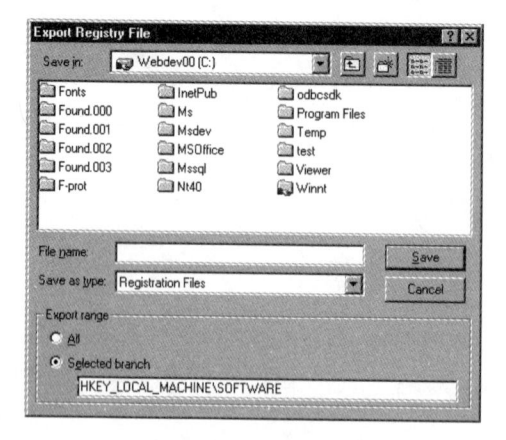

Figure 2.19 Exporting a branch of a Registry file

1. In the left-hand tree view, click to highlight the key you want to export. For example, HKEY_LOCAL_MACHINE\SOFTWARE.

2. From the Menu Bar, click Registry | Export Registry File... . The Export Registry File dialog box opens. The dialog assumes you want to export only part of the Registry file. Notice that in the "Export range," the Export Registry File dialog has checked the "Select branch" radio button and filled in the selected branch name for you.

3. Type the new filename for the exported file. For example, C:\temp\software.

4. Click OK.

The Registry Editor will create a scripting file of the HKEY_LOCAL_MACHINE\SOFTWARE branch of the Registry into a file called software.reg. You can view the file using Notepad. We discuss the syntax and semantics of the scripting file in the section "Registry File Scripting."

To export the whole Registry, follow these steps:

1. From the Registry Editor, click Registry | Export Registry File... from the Menu Bar. Do not highlight a key or subkey. The Export Registry File dialog box opens. The dialog assumes you want to export all of the Registry file. Notice in the "Export range" that the Export Registry File dialog has checked the "All" radio button.

2. Type the new filename for the exported file. For example, C:\temp\regfile.

3. Click OK.

Importing a Registry File

Warning: Importing a Registry file into the Registry is a permanent action. It cannot be undone.

To import a Registry file, follow these steps:

1. From the Menu Bar, click Registry | Import Registry File.... The Import Registry File dialog appears.

2. Locate and select the Registry file you want to import and click Enter. In this case, choose software.reg, which was created in the previous section. A progress dialog box appears while the file is being imported. See Figure 2.20.

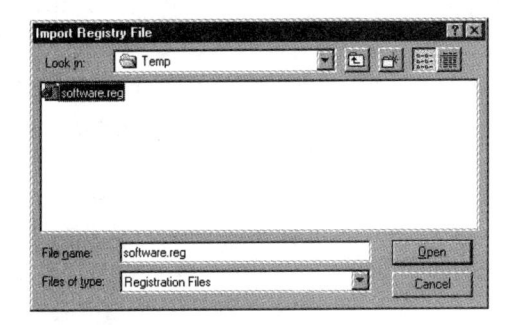

Figure 2.20 Importing a Registry file

3. After the file has been imported, a dialog box appears. If the import was successful, click OK to return to the Registry Editor. (If it was unsuccessful, then the imported file is corrupted.)

You do not need to highlight a specific key to be imported because the Registry file contains the names of the keys it will be creating and changing. Importing Registry files does not affect the keys and values currently in the Registry. Here are the rules that pertain to this:

- A key in the Registry that is not referenced in the imported Registry file will not be affected.

- A value in the Registry that is not referenced in the imported Registry file will not be affected.

- A key that is not in the Registry but is in the imported Registry file will be created in the original Registry.

- A name-value pair that is not in the Registry but is in the imported Registry file will be created in the original Registry.

- A name-value pair that is in the Registry and also in the imported Registry file will have its value set to the value in the imported Registry file.

- The child of a parent key that is in the Registry and in the imported Registry file will not be reset unless it also is in the imported Registry file.

Registry File Scripting

A **Registry scripting file** is a text file whose contents are of a particular syntax and semantics that the Registry Editor can read. It can be used to create Registry keys and name-value pairs. Since a Registry scripting file is a text file, users can read the keys and name-value pairs that the file contains. The Registry Editor can only create keys and name-value pairs with a Registry script; it cannot delete keys or name-values pairs. The extension for a Registry scripting file is .reg.

Creating a Registry Scripting File

You can create a Registry scripting file with the Registry Editor or by writing it by hand using a text editor. To create a scripting file with the Registry Editor, refer to the earlier section, "Exporting All or Part of a Registry File."

The syntax to write a scripting file by hand is not very involved. However, you need to ensure your syntax is correct because great damage to the operating system can result from changing keys in the Registry. In the following sections, we explain line by line how to create a scripting file.

File Header

The first line of the Registry scripting file is the header. It contains the version of the script that you intend to run; in this book, we discuss only version 4. To implement version 4 of your Registry scripting file, at the top of the file type

```
REGEDIT4
```

Creating a Key

Next, you want to create a key. Enclose the name of the key within brackets [ ] followed by an end-of-line (press Enter), as the following example shows:

```
REGEDIT4

[HKEY_LOCAL_MACHINE\SOFTWARE\Widget Software]
```

To create a second Registry key, you simply add a second line to the file:

```
REGEDIT4

[HKEY_LOCAL_MACHINE\SOFTWARE\Widget Software]
[HKEY_LOCAL_MACHINE\SOFTWARE\Widget
Software\Parameters]
```

The parent key does not need to exist for the subkey to be created. When the Registry Editor reads the scripting file, it will create both the parent key and the child key if they do not exist. So the previous example can be reduced to

```
REGEDIT4

[HKEY_LOCAL_MACHINE\SOFTWARE\Widget
Software\Parameters]
```

where both the Widget Software and Parameters keys will be created.

Setting the Default Value

Next, you set the default value for the keys. You do this by adding a line after the key that refers to the name of the default value as @. The delimiter is an equals sign (=), with the value following enclosed within quotation marks. For example, to set the default value of HKEY_LOCAL_MACHINE\SOFTWARE\Widget Software to Testing, you would write

```
REGEDIT4

[HKEY_LOCAL_MACHINE\SOFTWARE\Widget Software]
@="Testing"
```

If you don't define a default Registry setting, the default name-value pair still will be created, but the value will not be set. Every key must have a default value.

Creating a String Value

Creating a string value with Registry scripting is much like setting the default value, except you enter a name within quotation marks instead of using the @ symbol, as this example shows:

```
REGEDIT4

[HKEY_LOCAL_MACHINE\SOFTWARE\Widget Software]
@="Testing"
"WidgetName"="Widget"
```

You can add more name-value pairs by adding more lines after the line that creates the key. Each name-value pair is written on a separate single line.

Enclosing the names and the values within quotation marks ensures spaces are handled properly by the Registry Editor. That is, they are treated as spaces. But what happens when a quotation mark is part of the name or value? In this case, you want the quotation mark to be treated as a quotation mark. To ensure this occurs, you simply add a backward slash before the quotation mark, as follows:

```
REGEDIT4
```

```
[HKEY_LOCAL_MACHINE\SOFTWARE\Widget Software]
"WidgetContact"="Wayne \"Widget\" Berry"
```

Creating a DWORD Value

You also can declare a DWORD value with Registry scripting. To do this, you create a name-value pair declaration similarly to declaring a string, except you change the value to dword:<Number>, where Number is the value you want assigned to the DWORD. This example demonstrates:

```
REGEDIT4

[HKEY_LOCAL_MACHINE\SOFTWARE\Widget Software]
@="Testing"
"WidgetName"="Widget"
"WidgetCount"=dword:45
```

Note that 45 is a hexadecimal 45, which is equal to 69 in base ten. If your hexadecimal is very long, you can concatenate lines by using a backward slash \. Here is an example:

```
REGEDIT4

[HKEY_LOCAL_MACHINE\SOFTWARE\Widget Software]
@="Testing"
"WidgetName"="Widget"
"WidgetCount"=dword:45
"WidgetData"=hex:00,01,45,00,00,00,\
00,01,12,3E
```

Creating a Binary Value

Declaring a binary value is much like declaring a DWORD. You create a name-value pair declaration similarly to declaring a DWORD, except you change the value from dword to hex and give a comma-delimited set of hexadecimal numbers. Here is an example:

```
REGEDIT4
```

```
[HKEY_LOCAL_MACHINE\SOFTWARE\Widget Software]
@="Testing"
"WidgetName"="Widget"
"WidgetCount"=dword:45
"WidgetData"=hex:00,01,45
```

(Again, note that the 45 referred to in the scripting file is in hexadecimal; 69 is the decimal equivalent.)

Setting Many Keys at the Same Time

You can set any number of keys and/or name-value pairs. For each key, you make a key creation line, followed by as many name-value lines as needed. When keys follow each other, leave a blank line between each key. Here is an example:

```
REGEDIT4

[HKEY_LOCAL_MACHINE\SOFTWARE\Widget Software]
"WidgetContact"="Wayne \"Widget\" Berry"

[HKEY_LOCAL_MACHINE\SOFTWARE\Widget
Software\Parameters]
@="Testing"
"WidgetCount"=dword:01
```

Running a Registry Scripting File

You run a Registry scripting file by importing it into the Registry Editor and double-clicking it in Explorer. Or you can run it from a DOS command line.

We discussed importing the file with the Registry Editor in the previous section, "Importing a Registry File." To run the scripting file from Explorer, double-click the name of the file. The file must have a .reg extension. The operating system default mapping for .reg files is to call regedit.exe "%1".

To run a scripting file from the DOS command line, type

```
regedit <scriptname>.reg.
```

This command executes the file and brings up a dialog box that indicates whether the run was successful. Running scripting files at the command line can be helpful when doing batch jobs for installation programs.

Tip: When you are doing batch jobs and executing a scripting file from the command line, the dialog box that indicates whether the execution was successful or failed can be a problem. To suppress this dialog box, use the switch /s with the regedit.exe in the command line:

```
regedit /s <scriptname>.reg
```

What You Can't Do with the Registry Editor

This section's title might be a little misleading. After all, there are an infinite number of things you cannot do with the Registry Editor. For example, you cannot paint a flower with it. In this section, however, we talk about what you cannot do with the Registry that you can do with the Registry APIs and a little C code.

With the Registry Editor, you can create string, binary, and DWORD values. In the Registry APIs, these are called REG_SZ, REG_BINARY, and REG_DWORD, respectively. The following values, however, cannot be created with the Registry Editor; you must use Registry APIs instead:

- REG_DWORD_BIG_ENDIAN

- REG_EXPAND_SZ

- REG_LINK

- REG_MULTI_SZ

- REG_NONE

- REG_RESOURCE_LIST

Also, you cannot set the SECURITY parameter of a Registry key, make volatile keys, or load and unload hives with the Registry Editor. Instead, you use the APIs. We talk about the APIs in Chapter 3.

Chapter 3

Registry APIs

The Registry was designed to store application parameters that are to remain consistent between shutdowns and restarts of the operating system. A full set of APIs has been provided for manipulating the Registry. With them and with a bit of C Code, there is nothing you can't do to the Registry.

In this chapter, we discuss all the available APIs and give examples of each.

Opening and Closing a Parent Key

RegOpenKey
RegOpenKeyEx
RegCloseKey

To add a key, you first must open its parent key. All keys have a parent key. To open it, use RegOpenKey or RegOpenKeyEx. RegOpenKey has limited use. It was created when the Registry was first introduced. As the Registry became more popular and the number of applications that used it increased, RegOpenKeyEx was added. The "Ex" stands for expanded. RegOpenKey is retained to support applications that were written before RegOpenKeyEx was available. You should use RegOpenKeyEx.

After opening a key and performing all the modifications to it, you must close it to conserve system resources. Closing the key is done with RegCloseKey, which works with both RegOpenKey and RegOpenKeyEx.

RegOpenKey

RegOpenKey has the following three parameters:

1. The root key

2. The subkey to open

3. PHKEY, the handle to the application key

The first parameter is the root key, which may be one of the following:

- HKEY_CLASSES_ROOT

- HKEY_CURRENT_USER

- HKEY_LOCAL_MACHINE

- HKEY_USERS

The second parameter is the subkey to open. This can be considered a path from the root to the key you want to open. A typical subkey might look like this:

SYSTEM\\CurrentControlSet\\Services\\EventLog\\Application

Notice that the subkey is a **LPCTSTR.** LPCTSTR stands for a "long pointer to a constant string." Notice, too, that as with the Registry, a backward slash \ separates each key. However, there is no \ at the beginning of the string. (Also, if a backward slash is to appear as itself in a string, it must be written as a double backward slash, \\, to differentiate it from its use here in the single slash form.)

The third parameter is PHKEY. This is the handle to the application key and is used to perform modifications on the key.

Listing 3.1 shows example code for opening a key with RegOpenKey.

Listing 3.1

```
HKEY   hkKey;

RegOpenKey(
HKEY_LOCAL_MACHINE,
"SYSTEM\\CurrentControlSet\\Services\\EventLog
\\Application",
&hkKey
);
```

If RegOpenKey is successful in opening the key, it returns ERROR_ SUCCESS; otherwise, it returns an error value. It returns an error value if the key that you are trying to open doesn't exist in the Registry. To create a new key, you must use RegCreateKey, which is discussed later in this chapter.

With the extended Registry APIs comes a concept of security attributes. Security attributes enable the creator of a key to open the key even when another application has the key open. This is much like file access permissions. However, most applications do not share Registry keys, only certain types of OLE implementations, so security attributes are seldom used. RegOpenKeyEx specifies the access security to use. RegOpenKey, however, does not, so the security access is set at KEY_ALL_ACCESS.

RegOpenKeyEx

RegOpenKeyEx is more complex then RegOpenKey and performs more functions. It has the following five parameters:

1. The root key

2. Subkey to open

3. Reserved; must be 0

4. Security access to that key

5. PHKEY, the handle to the application key

The first parameter is the root key, which may be one of the following:

■ HKEY_CLASSES_ROOT

- HKEY_CURRENT_USER

- HKEY_LOCAL_MACHINE

- HKEY_USERS

The second parameter is the subkey to open. As with RegOpenKey, this can be considered a path from the root to the key you want to open. A typical subkey might look like this:

SYSTEM\\CurrentControlSet\\Services\\EventLog\\Application

Notice that the subkey is a LPCTSTR. **LPCTSTR** stands for a long pointer to a constant string. Notice, too, that as with the Registry, a backward slash \ separates each key. However, there is no \ at the beginning of the string. (Also, if a backward slash is to appear as itself in a string, it must be written as a double backward slash, \\, to differentiate it from its use here in the single slash form.)

The third parameter is reserved; it must be 0.

The fourth parameter is the security access to the key. Its value may be one of the following:

- KEY_ALL_ACCESS

  A combination of KEY_QUERY_VALUE, KEY_ENUMERATE_SUB_KEYS, KEY_NOTIFY, KEY_CREATE_SUB_KEY, KEY_CREATE_LINK, and KEY_SET_VALUE accesses

- KEY_CREATE_LINK

  Permission to create a symbolic link

- KEY_CREATE_SUB_KEY

  Permission to create subkeys

- KEY_ENUMERATE_SUB_KEYS

  Permission to enumerate subkeys

- KEY_EXECUTE

  Permission for read access

- KEY_NOTIFY

    Permission for change notification

- KEY_QUERY_VALUE

    Permission to query subkey data

- KEY_READ

    A combination of KEY_QUERY_VALUE, KEY_ENUMERATE_SUB_KEYS, and KEY_NOTIFY accesses

- KEY_SET_VALUE

    Permission to set subkey data

- KEY_WRITE

    A combination of KEY_SET_VALUE and KEY_CREATE_SUB_KEY accesses

You can combine the values with a bitwise OR. If you don't know what to use, choose KEY_ALL_ACCESS. Most of the other security attributes are reserved for Registry keys where more than one DLL is writing to the Registry at one time.

The fifth parameter is PHKEY. This is the handle to the application key and is used to perform modifications on the key.

Like RegOpenKey, RegOpenKeyEx returns an ERROR_SUCCESS for a successful opening of the key and an error value otherwise. It returns an error if the key you are trying to open doesn't exist in the Registry. To create a new key, you must use RegCreateKey, which is discussed later in the chapter.

Listing 3.2 shows some example code for opening a key with RegOpenKeyEx.

Listing 3.2

```
HKEY  hkKey;

if (RegOpenKeyEx(
HKEY_LOCAL_MACHINE,
"SYSTEM\\CurrentControlSet\\Services\\EventLog
\\Application",
```

```
0,
KEY_ALL_ACCESS,
&hkKey)!=ERROR_SUCCESS)
{
// TODO : Add Error Handling Code
}
```

RegCloseKey

After opening a key and performing all the modifications to it, you must close it so as to conserve system resources. Closing the key is done with RegCloseKey, which works with both RegOpenKey and RegOpenKeyEx.

RegCloseKey takes one parameter: the key handle that was returned from RegOpenKey or RegOpenKeyEx.

Listing 3.3 shows some example code for closing a key with RegCloseKey. It is a rewrite of Listing 3.2 that shows how to conserve system resources.

Listing 3.3
```
HKEY   hkKey=NULL;

if (RegOpenKeyEx(
HKEY_LOCAL_MACHINE,
"SYSTEM\\CurrentControlSet\\Services\\EventLog
\\Application",
0,
KEY_ALL_ACCESS,
&hkKey)!=ERROR_SUCCESS)
{
// TODO : Add Error Handling Code
}

if (hkKey)
RegCloseKey(hkKey);
```

Creating Keys

RegCreateKey
RegCreateKeyEx

There are two APIs for creating keys: RegCreateKey and RegCreateKeyEx. RegCreateKey was the first API used to create a key. With the advent of 32-bit programming, RegCreateKeyEx was added to provide additional functionality. RegCreateKey does the job in most cases and is easier to program, so it is tempting to use it instead of RegCreateKeyEx. However, you should use RegCreateKeyEx because RegCreateKey might not be supported in the future.

RegCreateKey

RegCreateKey creates a subkey within a parent key. The secret to creating a key is to have first opened the parent key with either RegOpenKey or RegOpenKeyEx. You must open the parent key using either KEY_CREATE_SUB_KEY security access or a security access that covers the KEY_CREATE_SUB_KEY security access, such as KEY_ALL_ACCESS.

RegCreateKey has the following three parameters:

1. The root key

2. The subkey of the root key in which you want to create the key

3. PHKEY, the handle to the key

The first parameter is the root key, which may be one of the following:

- HKEY_CLASSES_ROOT

- HKEY_CURRENT_USER

- HKEY_LOCAL_MACHINE

- HKEY_USERS

The second parameter is the subkey of the root key in which you want to create the key. A typical subkey might look like this:

SYSTEM\\CurrentControlSet\\Services\\EventLog\\Application
\\TestApp

where TestApp is the key being created. You may create more than one
subkey at a time by specifying a string like this:

SYSTEM\\CurrentControlSet\\Services\\EventLog\\Application
\\TestApp\\Parameters

which will create both the TestApp and the Parameters keys.

The third parameter is PHKEY, the handle to the key. It is used later to
modify the key.

If creating the key is successful, RegCreateKey returns an ERROR_
SUCCESS; otherwise it returns an error code. The key is opened on creation,
so you needn't open it again with RegOpenKey or RegOpenKeyEx. The
security access is KEY_ALL_ACCESS by default. Remember to close the
key using RegCloseKey.

Listing 3.4 shows example code for creating a key using RegOpenKey.

Listing 3.4

```
HKEY  hkKey=NULL;

if (RegCreateKey(
HKEY_LOCAL_MACHINE,
"SYSTEM\\CurrentControlSet\\Services\\EventLog
\\Application\\TestApp",
&hkKey)!=ERROR_SUCCESS)
{
// TODO : Add Error Handling Code
}

if (hkKey)
RegCloseKey(hkKey);
```

RegCreateKeyEx

RegCreateKeyEx is a lot like RegCreateKey, except it takes more functions and therefore offers you more control. RegCreateKeyEx lets you

create a key that is opened with a specific security access rather than the default access, like RegCreateKey. It also allows you to open the key if it exists or create a key with the new attributes. Another feature, specific to Windows NT only, lets you create a key that either is permanent in the register or will be deleted when NT is restarted. RegCreateKeyEx should be used for all 32-bit applications.

RegCreateKeyEx has the following nine parameters:

1. The root key

2. The subkey

3. A reserved DWORD, which must be 0

4. A NULL-terminated string that contains the name of the class or object type of the key

5. The specified special options for the key being created

6. The type of security access the new key gets

7. The security attribute

8. A pointer to a key handle

9. A long pointer to a DWORD

The first parameter is the root key, which may be one of the following:

■ HKEY_CLASSES_ROOT

■ HKEY_CURRENT_USER

■ HKEY_LOCAL_MACHINE

■ HKEY_USERS

The second parameter is the subkey. It may be one of the following:

■ A new subkey that you want to create

■ An existing key whose attributes you want to change

■ An existing key that you want to ensure will exist but do not want to change

A typical subkey might look like this:

SYSTEM\\CurrentControlSet\\Services\\EventLog\\Application
\\TestApp

where TestApp is the key being created. You may create more then one subkey at a time by specifying a string like this:

SYSTEM\\CurrentControlSet\\Services\\EventLog\\Application
\\TestApp\\Parameters

The third parameter is a reserved DWORD; it must be 0.

The fourth parameter is a NULL-terminated string that contains the name of the class or object type of the key. This parameter is not a pointer to the object; it is just the object name.

Note: Most Registry viewers do not allow you to view the class of the key.

The fifth parameter is the specified special options for the key being created. You may have three types of keys in Windows NT and only one type in Windows 95, as follows:

1. Nonvolatile key

   This is the most common type of Registry key and the only one sup-ported by Windows 95. A key of this type is a permanent part of the Registry; it doesn't go away when the operating system is shut down.

2. Volatile key

   A volatile key is supported only under Windows NT. Volatile keys exist only until the system is restarted. If the key already exists as a nonvolatile key, then this parameter is ignored. Under Windows 95, if nonvolatile is specified then a volatile key is created and RegCreateKeyEx returns ERROR_SUCCESS.

3. Backup or restore key

   This key is available so that NT users with backup and restore permis-sions can back up the register. It ignores the next parameter—the access mask—and opens the key with permissions to back up or restore the key based on the thread. If the thread has SE_BACKUP_NAME privilege, then the key is created with ACCESS_SYSTEM_SECURITY and KEY_READ permissions. If the thread has SE_RESTORE_NAME, the key is opened with ACCESS_SYSTEM_SECURITY and KEY_WRITE permissions. Windows 95 does not support the backup or restore key.

Following are the predefined constants used to select the special options for creating a key:

- REG_OPTION_NON_VOLATILE

- REG_OPTION_VOLATILE

- REG_OPTION_BACKUP_RESTORE

The sixth parameter is the type of security access the new key gets. It may be one of the following:

- KEY_ALL_ACCESS

  A combination of KEY_QUERY_VALUE, KEY_ENUMERATE_SUB_KEYS, KEY_NOTIFY, KEY_CREATE_SUB_KEY, KEY_CREATE_LINK, and KEY_SET_VALUE accesses

- KEY_CREATE_LINK

  Permission to create a symbolic link

- KEY_CREATE_SUB_KEY

  Permission to create subkeys

- KEY_ENUMERATE_SUB_KEYS

  Permission to enumerate subkeys

- KEY_EXECUTE

  Permission for read access

- KEY_NOTIFY

  Permission for change notification

- KEY_QUERY_VALUE

  Permission to query subkey data

- KEY_READ

  A combination of KEY_QUERY_VALUE, KEY_ENUMERATE_SUB_KEYS, and KEY_NOTIFY accesses

- KEY_SET_VALUE

  Permission to set subkey data

- KEY_WRITE

  A combination of KEY_SET_VALUE and KEY_CREATE_SUB_KEY accesses

If you don't know what to use for the sixth parameter, choose KEY_ALL_ACCESS. Most of the other security attributes are reserved for Registry keys where more than one DLL is writing to the Registry at one time.

The seventh parameter is the security attribute. In Windows 95, the security descriptor is ignored, so set it to NULL. In Windows NT, the attribute determines whether the key handle can be inherited by the child processes of the process that created the key. The security attribute is in a formal parameter structure called SECURITY_ATTRIBUTES. The structure looks like this:

```
typedef struct _SECURITY_ATTRIBUTES { // sa
  DWORD nLength;
  LPVOID lpSecurityDescriptor;
  BOOL  bInheritHandle;
} SECURITY_ATTRIBUTES;
```

To ensure the child process can use the key handle, create a SECURITY_ATTRIBUTES like this, passing &saSecurityAttributes as the security attribute:

```
SECURITY_ATTRIBUTES  saSecurityAttributes;
```

```
saSecurityAttributes.nLength =
sizeof(SECURITY_ATTRIBUTES);
saSecurityAttributes.lpSecurityDescriptor = NULL;
saSecurityAttributes.bInheritHandle = TRUE;
```

If you don't care whether the child process can inherit the key handle, then set the security attribute to NULL. If in Windows NT the security attribute is NULL, then the default security attribute that is used is the one that prevents the child process from using the created key handle.

The eighth parameter is a pointer to a key handle. When the key is created successfully, the pointer will point to the newly created key handle. This handle can be used to represent the created key in other calls.

The ninth and final parameter is a long pointer to a DWORD. When the key is created successfully, the DWORD will be either

- REG_CREATED_NEW_KEY, if a new key was created, or

- REG_OPENED_EXISTING_KEY, if the key already existed and was opened without being changed.

Remember that when a key is created, it also is opened. So close the key when you are done with it.

If RegCreateKeyEx completed successfully, it returns ERROR_SUCCESS; otherwise, it returns an error value.

Listing 3.5 shows example code to demonstrate the use of RegCreateKeyEx.

Listing 3.5
```
HKEY      hkKey=NULL;
DWORD dwDisposition;

SECURITY_ATTRIBUTES saSecurityAttributes;

saSecurityAttributes.nLength =
sizeof(SECURITY_ATTRIBUTES);
saSecurityAttributes.lpSecurityDescriptor = NULL;
saSecurityAttributes.bInheritHandle = TRUE;

if (RegCreateKeyEx(
HKEY_LOCAL_MACHINE,
```

```
"SYSTEM\\CurrentControlSet\\Services\\EventLog
\\Application\\TestApp",
0,
"",
REG_OPTION_NON_VOLATILE,
KEY_ALL_ACCESS,
& saSecurityAttributes,
&hkKey,
&dwDisposition)!=ERROR_SUCCESS)
{
// TODO : Add Error Handling Code
}

if (hkKey)
RegCloseKey(hkKey);
```

Setting the Value of a Key

RegSetValue
RegSetValueEx

RegSetValue and RegSetValueEx sets the value of a key in the Registry. RegSetValue should be used only with 16-bit applications running under Windows 3.1. Win32 applications should use RegSetValueEx. RegSetValue has a limited use for Win32 applications because the values it creates can only be text strings and are not named. RegSetValue sets the value of the key's default only.

To create multiple name-value pairs under one Registry key, you must use RegSetValueEx.

RegSetValue

RegSetValue has five parameters. The first two depend on how you want to indicate for which key you want to create a value. There are two ways:

1. Obtain a pointer to a key by calling RegOpenKey, RegOpenKeyEx, RegCreateKey, or RegCreateKeyEx. Then use that pointer as the first parameter and NULL as the second parameter to RegSetValue.

2. Use the root key as the first parameter. As the second parameter, use a string that indicates the key to use. Following are the root keys:

- HKEY_CLASSES_ROOT

- HKEY_CURRENT_USER

- HKEY_LOCAL_MACHINE

- HKEY_USERS

The other parameters are as follows:

3. The type of value to create. This must be REG_SZ. Other types of values can be created using RegSetValueEx.

4. A long pointer to a NULL-terminated string that contains the value assigned the key.

5. The length of that string. The length doesn't include the NULL-terminated string.

Listing 3.5 shows example code for setting a value on a key that is already open.

Listing 3.5
```
HKEY   hkKey=NULL;

if (RegCreateKey(
HKEY_LOCAL_MACHINE,
"SYSTEM\\CurrentControlSet\\Services\\EventLog
\\Application\\TestApp",
&hkKey)!=ERROR_SUCCESS)
{
// TODO : Add Error Handling Code
}

if (RegSetValue(hkKey,NULL,REG_SZ,"Foo", _tcslen("Foo") )
!= ERROR_SUCCESS)
{
// TODO : Add Error Handling Code
}
```

```
if (hkKey)
RegCloseKey(hkKey);
```

Listing 3.6 shows example code for setting the value on a key without opening the key.

Listing 3.6
```
if (RegSetValue(HKEY_LOCAL_MACHINE,
"SYSTEM\\CurrentControlSet\\Services\\EventLog
\\Application\\TestApp", REG_SZ,"Foo",
_tcslen("Foo") )!=ERROR_SUCCESS)
{
// TODO : Add Error Handling Code
}
```

Both examples create exactly the same key.

If a key indicated in the second parameter doesn't exist, it is created. Hence, you can set the value and the key all in one call to RegSetValue.

If the key is already open when RegSetValue is called, then that key must have been opened with either KEY_SET_VALUE access or an access value that includes KEY_SET_VALUE access, such as KEY_ALL_ACCESS. By default, RegCreateKey in the previous example has KEY_ALL_ACCESS access.

If RegCreateKey completes successfully, it returns ERROR_SUCCESS; otherwise, it returns an error value.

RegSetValueEx

RegSetValueEx is an extended version of RegSetValue. In RegSetValueEx, you can set value to types other than REG_SZ. Unlike with RegSetValue, when using RegSetValueEx you must first open the key for which you want to set the value.

An important feature of RegSetValueEx is that, unlike with RegSetValue, you can create name-value pairs within a single key. This is because of changes to the Registry structure between the Windows 3.1 and the 32-bit Windows operating systems.

RegSetValueEx has the following six parameters:

1. A handle to a key or a root key

2. The string indicating the name of the name-value pair that is to be set in the key

3. Reserved; should be set to 0

4. The type of value that is to be set

5. The address of the data that represents the value

6. The length of the value data

The first parameter of RegSetValueEx is either a handle to a key you opened by calling RegOpenKey, RegOpenKeyEx, RegCreateKey, or RegCreateKeyEx or one of the following root keys:

- HKEY_CLASSES_ROOT

- HKEY_CURRENT_USER

- HKEY_LOCAL_MACHINE

- HKEY_USERS

The second parameter is the string that indicates the name of the name-value pair to be set in the key. If a pair doesn't appear with the name of the string, another pair is created with the RegSetValueEx information. This is how multiple name-value pairs are created in a single key. If you want to set the default value of the key, you must set the second parameter to NULL and the third parameter to REG_SZ.

The third parameter is reserved; it should be set to 0.

The fourth parameter is the type of value that is to be set. The parameter may be one of the following constants:

- REG_BINARY

  Binary data in any form

- REG_DWORD

  A 32-bit number

- REG_DWORD_LITTLE_ENDIAN

  A 32-bit number in little-endian format (same as REG_DWORD). In little-endian format, the most significant byte of a word is the high-order word. This is the most common format for computers running Windows NT and Windows 95.

- REG_DWORD_BIG_ENDIAN

  A 32-bit number in big-endian format. In big-endian format, the most significant byte of a word is the low-order word.

- REG_EXPAND_SZ

  A NULL-terminated string that contains unexpanded references to environment variables (for example, "%PATH%"). It will be a Unicode or ANSI string, depending on whether you use the Unicode function or ANSI function.

- REG_LINK

  A Unicode symbolic link

- REG_MULTI_SZ

  An array of NULL-terminated strings, terminated by two NULL characters

- REG_NONE

  No defined value type

- REG_RESOURCE_LIST

  A device-driver resource list

- REG_SZ

  A NULL-terminated string. It will be a Unicode or ANSI string, depending on whether you use the Unicode function or ANSI function.

  The fifth parameter is the address of the data that represents the value. The sixth parameter is the length of the value data. If the type of value to be set is REG_SZ, REG_EXPAND_SZ, or REG_MULTI_SZ, then the length must include the NULL-terminated string. This is unlike RegSetValue, where the length didn't include the NULL-terminated string.

If you are using an already-open key when calling RegSetValueEx, then that key must have been opened with either KEY_SET_VALUE access or an access value that includes KEY_SET_VALUE access, such as KEY_ALL_ACCESS.

If KEY_SET_VALUE completes successfully, it returns ERROR_SUCCESS; otherwise, it returns an error value.

Listing 3.7 shows an example of creating multiple name-value pairs within a single key, with each pair having a different value type.

Listing 3.7

```
HKEY hkKey=NULL;
DWORD dwDisposition;
DWORD dwFoo=10;
TCHAR   lpStringList[][5]= {
"Foo1","Foo2","Foo3","\0"};
DWORD   dwListSize=sizeof(lpStringList);

if (RegCreateKeyEx(
HKEY_LOCAL_MACHINE,
"SYSTEM\\CurrentControlSet\\Services\\EventLog
\\Application\\TestApp",
0,
"",
REG_OPTION_NON_VOLATILE,
KEY_ALL_ACCESS,
NULL,
&hkKey,
&dwDisposition)!=ERROR_SUCCESS)
{
// TODO : Add Error Handling Code
}

// Setting the Default Value for the Key
if (RegSetValueEx(
hkKey,
NULL,
0,
```

```
REG_SZ,
(CONST BYTE *)"Foo",
_tcslen("Foo")+1
)!=ERROR_SUCCESS)
{
// TODO : Add Error Handling Code
}

// Create a name value pair with a name of FooString,
// with a type of REG_SZ
if (RegSetValueEx(
hkKey,
"FooString",
0,
REG_SZ,
(CONST BYTE *)"Foo",
_tcslen("Foo")+1
)!=ERROR_SUCCESS)
{
// TODO : Add Error Handling Code
}

// Create a name value pair with a name of FooPath,
// with a type of REG_EXPAND_SZ
if (RegSetValueEx(
hkKey,
"FooPath",
0,
REG_EXPAND_SZ,
(CONST BYTE *)"%%PATH%%",
_tcslen("%%PATH%%")+1
)!=ERROR_SUCCESS)
{
// TODO : Add Error Handling Code
}

// Create a name value pair with a name of FooDWORD,
// with a type of REG_DWORD
```

```
if (RegSetValueEx(
hkKey,
"FoODWORD",
0,
REG_DWORD,
(CONST BYTE *)&dwFoo,
sizeof(DWORD)
)!=ERROR_SUCCESS)
{
// TODO : Add Error Handling Code
}

// Create a name value pair with a name of FooStrings,
// with a type of REG_MULTI_SZ
if (RegSetValueEx(
hkKey,
"FooStrings",
0,
REG_MULTI_SZ,
(CONST BYTE *)lpStringList,
dwListSize
)!=ERROR_SUCCESS)
{
// TODO : Add Error Handling Code
}

if (hkKey)
RegCloseKey(hkKey);
```

Deleting a Key and Its Values

RegDeleteKey

RegDeleteKey deletes a key and all of its values. In Windows 95, it deletes all the subkeys of the specific key. In Windows NT, you cannot delete a key if it has subkeys.

RegDeleteKey has the following two parameters:

1. An open key handle or one of the root keys

2. A NULL-terminated string that indicates which subkey to delete

The first parameter is an open key handle or one of the following root keys:

- HKEY_CLASSES_ROOT

- HKEY_CURRENT_USER

- HKEY_LOCAL_MACHINE

- HKEY_USERS

The second parameter is a NULL-terminated string that indicates which subkey to delete. The string may not be NULL.

There are two ways to delete a key:

1. Choose the correct root key for the first parameter and then indicate the full path of the subkey in the second parameter.

2. Open the parent key with RegOpenKey or RegOpenKeyEx and then pass in the open key handle as the first parameter. If you pass in the open key handle, then you must set the second parameter as the name of the child key.

Listing 3.8 shows an example of using a root key to delete a subkey.

Listing 3.8

```
if (RegDeleteKey(
HKEY_LOCAL_MACHINE,
"SYSTEM\\CurrentControlSet\\Services\\EventLog
\\Application\\TestApp"
))
{
// TODO : Add Error Handling Code
}
```

Listing 3.9 shows an example of using an open key handle to delete a key.

Listing 3.9

```
HKEY  hkKey=NULL;

if (RegOpenKeyEx(
HKEY_LOCAL_MACHINE,
"SYSTEM\\CurrentControlSet\\Services\\EventLog
\\Application",
0,
KEY_ALL_ACCESS,
&hkKey)!=ERROR_SUCCESS)
{
// TODO : Add Error Handling Code
}

if (RegDeleteKey(hkKey,"TestApp"))
{
// TODO : Add Error Handling Code
}

if (hkKey)
RegCloseKey(hkKey);
```

Both examples delete exactly the same key.

You cannot delete a subkey of a parent that has been opened with RegCreateKey or RegCreateKeyEx and not closed using RegCloseKey. Always use RegOpenKey or RegOpenKeyEx to open the parent key.

If RegDeleteKey completes successfully, it returns ERROR_SUCCESS; otherwise, it returns an error value.

Flushing Registry Changes to Disk

RegFlushKey

RegFlushKey flushes Registry changes to the disk. Calling this function is usually not necessary because the Registry flushes itself during idle times or system shutdown. It needs to be called only when you want to ensure that changes get to the disk before you start executing the rest of the code. RegFlushKey does not return until all the changes have been written to the disk. Its only parameter is a handle to an open key or one of the following root keys:

- HKEY_CLASSES_ROOT

- HKEY_CURRENT_USER

- HKEY_LOCAL_MACHINE

- HKEY_USERS

Listing 3.10 shows an example of using RegFlushKey.

Listing 3.10

```
HKEY  hkKey=NULL;

if (RegCreateKey(
HKEY_LOCAL_MACHINE,
"SYSTEM\\CurrentControlSet\\Services\\EventLog
\\Application\\TestApp",
&hkKey)!=ERROR_SUCCESS)
{
// TODO : Add Error Handling Code
}

if (RegFlushKey(hkKey))
{
// TODO : Add Error Handling Code
}

if (hkKey)
RegCloseKey(hkKey);
```

If RegFlushKey completes successfully, it returns ERROR_SUCCESS; otherwise, it returns an error value.

Opening a Registry Key on Another Computer

RegConnectRegistry

RegConnectRegistry opens a Registry key on a remote computer. It has the following three parameters:

1. The name of the remote computer

2. An HKEY value

3. A pointer to a key handle

The first parameter is the name of the remote computer. The string's format must be \\COMPUTERNAME. If the parameter is NULL, then the local machine is used.

The second parameter is one of the following, which indicates the root key on the remote machine:

■ HKEY_LOCAL_MACHINE

■ HKEY_USERS

In this call, you cannot use HKEY_CLASSES_ROOT or HKEY_CURRENT_USER.

The third parameter is a pointer to a key handle, which in turn obtains the key handle of the Registry key on the local machine.

If RegConnectRegistry completes successfully, it returns ERROR_SUCCESS; otherwise, it returns an error value.

Note that you may open only the root keys on the remote machine. However, you can open a subkey with another call to RegOpenKeyEx using the key handle from RegConnectRegistry.

Listing 3.11 shows example code for using RegConnectRegistry.

Listing 3.11

```
HKEY  hkKey=NULL;
HKEY  hkKey2=NULL;

if (RegConnectRegistry(
"\\\\TESTMACHINE",
HKEY_LOCAL_MACHINE ,
```

```
&hkKey)!=ERROR_SUCCESS)
{
// TODO : Add Error Handling Code
}

if (RegOpenKeyEx(
hkKey,
"SYSTEM\\CurrentControlSet\\Services\\EventLog
\\Application",
0,
KEY_ALL_ACCESS,
& hkKey2)!=ERROR_SUCCESS)
{
// TODO : Add Error Handling Code
}

if (hkKey)
RegCloseKey(hkKey);

if (hkKey2)
RegCloseKey(hkKey2);
```

Obtaining the Default Value

RegQueryValue
RegQueryValueEx

RegQueryValue and RegQueryValueEx get the value from the default value in the Registry key. RegQueryValue should be used with 16-bit applications. You should use RegQueryValueEx with Win32 applications to get the values of other name-value pairs in the key.

RegQueryValue

RegQueryValue has the following four parameters:

1. An open key handle or one of the root keys

2. A NULL-terminated string that indicates which subkey to query

3. A pointer to an already-allocated memory that will hold the key's value

4. A pointer to a long value

The first parameter to RegQueryValue is an open key handle or one of the following root keys:

- HKEY_CLASSES_ROOT

- HKEY_CURRENT_USER

- HKEY_LOCAL_MACHINE

- HKEY_USERS

The second parameter is a NULL-terminated string that indicates which subkey to query. The string may be NULL if you are using an already-open key as the first parameter.

There are two ways to indicate which key to query:

1. Choose the correct root key for the first parameter and then indicate the full path of the subkey in the second parameter.

2. Open the key with RegOpenKey or RegOpenKeyEx and then set the second parameter to NULL.

The third parameter is the pointer to an already-allocated memory area where RegQueryValue will put the value of the key. Enough memory should be allocated to hold the string, including the terminating NULL character.

The fourth parameter is a pointer to a long value. When the function is called, the long value should indicate the size of the buffer in the third parameter, including the terminating NULL character. When the function returns, the long value is set to the size of the value, including the NULL character.

Listing 3.12 shows example code for querying the default value in a key using a root key.

Listing 3.12
```
TCHAR lpszValue[10];
LONG    lValueSize=10;
```

```
if(RegQueryValue(
HKEY_LOCAL_MACHINE,
"SYSTEM\\CurrentControlSet\\Services\\EventLog
\\Application\\TestApp",
lpszValue,
&lValueSize
)!=ERROR_SUCCESS)
{
// TODO Handle Error
}
```

Listing 3.13 shows how to query a key using an already-open key.

Listing 3.13
```
HKEY  hkKey=NULL;
TCHAR lpszValue[10];
LONG  lValueSize=10;

if (RegOpenKey(
HKEY_LOCAL_MACHINE,
"SYSTEM\\CurrentControlSet\\Services\\EventLog
\\Application\\TestApp",
&hkKey
)!=ERROR_SUCCESS)
{
// TODO Handle Error
}

if(RegQueryValue(
hkKey,
NULL,
lpszValue,
&lValueSize
)!=ERROR_SUCCESS)
{
// TODO Handle Error
}
```

```
if (hkKey)
RegCloseKey(hkKey);
```

When the length of the value is not known, you can query the key twice, the first time to learn the size of the value and the second time to get the value. Listing 3.14 shows an example of this technique.

Listing 3.14

```
HKEY   hkKey=NULL;
LPTSTR lpszValue;
LONG   lValueSize=10;

if (RegOpenKey(
HKEY_LOCAL_MACHINE,
"SYSTEM\\CurrentControlSet\\Services\\EventLog
\\Application\\TestApp",
&hkKey
)!=ERROR_SUCCESS)
{
// TODO Handle Error
}

if(RegQueryValue(
hkKey,
NULL,
NULL,
&lValueSize
)!=ERROR_SUCCESS)
{
// TODO Handle Error
}
else
{

lpszValue=new TCHAR[lValueSize];

if(RegQueryValue(
hkKey,
```

```
NULL,
lpszValue,
&lValueSize
)!=ERROR_SUCCESS)
{
// TODO Handle Error
}

delete lpszValue;
}

if (hkKey)
RegCloseKey(hkKey);
```

When NULL is passed in as the third parameter, RegQueryValue does not try to query the value. Instead, it returns the size of the value in the long value of the fourth parameter.

RegQueryValueEx

RegQueryValueEx is an extension of RegQueryValue. With RegQueryValueEx, you can query the value of a specific key by value name. Unlike with RegQueryValue, you can use RegQueryValueEx to query any value data type. Also unlike with RegQueryValue, when using RegQueryValueEx you must first open the key whose value you want to set.

An important difference between RegQueryValueEx and RegQueryValue is that you can only query the values of name-value pairs with RegQueryValueEx.

RegQueryValueEx has the following six parameters:

1. A handle to a key you opened or one of the root keys

2. The string indicating the name of the name-value pair that is to be set in the key

3. Reserved; should be set to NULL

4. The type of value to be set

5. An address where memory has been allocated to receive the data being queried

6. A pointer to a DWORD

The first parameter is either a handle to a key you opened by calling RegOpenKey, RegOpenKeyEx, RegCreateKey, or RegCreateKeyEx or one of the following root keys:

- HKEY_CLASSES_ROOT

- HKEY_CURRENT_USER

- HKEY_LOCAL_MACHINE

- HKEY_USERS

The second parameter of RegQueryValueEx is the string indicating the name of the name-value pair that is to be set in the key.

The third parameter is reserved; it should be set to NULL. If you want to query the default value of the key, you must make the second parameter NULL and set the third parameter to REG_SZ.

The fourth parameter is a pointer to a DWORD, which is set to the value type of the particular name-value pair. The type can be any one of the following:

- REG_BINARY

    Binary data in any form

- REG_DWORD

    A 32-bit number

- REG_DWORD_LITTLE_ENDIAN

    A 32-bit number in little-endian format (same as REG_DWORD). In little-endian format, the most significant byte of a word is the high-order word. This is the most common format for computers running Windows NT and Windows 95.

- REG_DWORD_BIG_ENDIAN

  A 32-bit number in big-endian format. In big-endian format, the most significant byte of a word is the low-order word.

- REG_EXPAND_SZ

  A NULL-terminated string that contains unexpanded references to environment variables (for example, "%PATH%"). It will be a Unicode or ANSI string, depending on whether you use the Unicode function or ANSI function.

- REG_LINK

  A Unicode symbolic link

- REG_MULTI_SZ

  An array of NULL-terminated strings, terminated by two NULL characters.

- REG_NONE

  No defined value type

- REG_RESOURCE_LIST

  A device-driver resource list

- REG_SZ

  A NULL-terminated string. It will be a Unicode or ANSI string, depending on whether you use the Unicode function or ANSI function.

The fifth parameter is an address of memory that has been allocated to receive the data being queried.

The sixth parameter is a pointer to a DWORD. When RegQueryValueEx is called, the DWORD should indicate the size of the buffer in the fifth parameter. If the value type is REG_SZ, REG_MULTI_SZ, or REG_EXPAND_SZ, then the DWORD should include the terminating NULL character. When the function returns, the long value is set to the size of the value, including the NULL character if the value type is REG_SZ, REG_MULTI_SZ, or REG_EXPAND_SZ.

If RegQueryValueEx completes successfully, it returns ERROR_SUCCESS; otherwise, it returns an error value.

The key being queried must have been opened with KEY_QUERY_VALUE. If you query a value stored under REG_EXPAND_SZ, the value will not be expanded at the time of the query. You will need to use a function called ExpandEnvironmentStrings to expand the value. We do not discuss that function in this book.

Listing 3.15 shows some example code for querying with RegQueryValueEx. Before running List 3.15, you need to run Listing 3.7, which creates the name-value pairs to query.

Listing 3.15

```
HKEY hkKey=NULL;

DWORD dwFoo=10;
TCHAR lpszFooPathValue[10];
TCHAR lpszDefaultValue[5];
TCHAR lpszFooStringValue[5];

DWORD cbData;
DWORD dwValueType;

TCHAR lpStringList[][5]= { "1234","1234","1234","\0"};
DWORD dwListSize=sizeof(lpStringList);

LONG lErrorCode;

// Open a Handle to the Key

if (lErrorCode=RegOpenKeyEx(
HKEY_LOCAL_MACHINE,
"SYSTEM\\CurrentControlSet\\Services\\EventLog
\\Application\\TestApp",
0,
KEY_QUERY_VALUE,
&hkKey)!=ERROR_SUCCESS)
{
// TODO : Add Error Handling Code
}
else
{
```

```
// Query the Default Value

cbData=5;

if (RegQueryValueEx(
hkKey,
NULL,
NULL,
&dwValueType,
(LPBYTE)lpszDefaultValue,
&cbData
)!=ERROR_SUCCESS)
{
// TODO : Add Error Handling Code
}


// Query FooString which is a REG_SZ

cbData=5;

if (RegQueryValueEx(
hkKey,
"FooString",
NULL,
&dwValueType,
(LPBYTE)lpszFooStringValue,
&cbData
)!=ERROR_SUCCESS)
{
// TODO : Add Error Handling Code
}


// Query FooPath which is a REG_EXPAND_SZ

cbData=10;

if (RegQueryValueEx(
hkKey,
```

```
"FooPath",
NULL,
&dwValueType,
(LPBYTE)lpszFooPathValue,
&cbData
)!=ERROR_SUCCESS)
{
// TODO : Add Error Handling Code
}


// Query FooDWORD which is a REG_DWORD

cbData=sizeof(DWORD);

if (RegQueryValueEx(
hkKey,
"FooDWORD",
NULL,
&dwValueType,
(LPBYTE)&dwFoo,
&cbData
)!=ERROR_SUCCESS)
{
// TODO : Add Error Handling Code
}

// Query FooDWORD which is a REG_MULTI_SZ

cbData=dwListSize;

if (RegQueryValueEx(
hkKey,
"FooStrings",
NULL,
&dwValueType,
(LPBYTE)lpStringList,
&cbData
)!=ERROR_SUCCESS)
```

```
{
// TODO : Add Error Handling Code
}

RegCloseKey(hkKey);
}
```

Listing 3.15 is a little too simple for production applications. Notice that we allocate enough room ahead of time to get "FooStrings." We even know the type of array it is in. Production applications may not know this information. By making the fifth parameter NULL, RegQueryValueEx doesn't try to fill in the data; it just returns the data size in the sixth parameter. By knowing the data size, we can allocate enough room to hold the value and then query again to get the value. Listing 3.16 shows an example using "FooStrings," where the string structure of the REG_MULTI_SZ name-value pair is unknown.

Listing 3.16
```
HKEY hkKey=NULL;
DWORD cbData;
DWORD dwValueType;
LPTSTR lpStringList;
DWORD dwListSize=sizeof(lpStringList);
LONG lErrorCode;

// Open a Handle to the Key

if (lErrorCode=RegOpenKeyEx(
HKEY_LOCAL_MACHINE,
"SYSTEM\\CurrentControlSet\\Services\\EventLog
\\Application\\TestApp",
0,
KEY_QUERY_VALUE,
&hkKey)!=ERROR_SUCCESS)
{
// TODO : Add Error Handling Code
}
```

```
else
{
// Query the Name-Value Pair for the Size of the Value
if (RegQueryValueEx(
hkKey,
"FooStrings",
NULL,
&dwValueType,
NULL,
&cbData
)!=ERROR_SUCCESS)
{
// TODO : Add Error Handling Code
}

// Allocate enough room for the value
lpStringList = new TCHAR[cbData];

// Query the Name-Value Pair for the Value
if (RegQueryValueEx(
hkKey,
"FooStrings",
NULL,
&dwValueType,
(LPBYTE)lpStringList,
&cbData
)!=ERROR_SUCCESS)
{
// TODO : Add Error Handling Code
}
delete lpStringList;
RegCloseKey(hkKey);
```

If you already know the value type you are querying, then you don't
need to supply a DWORD in the fourth parameter; you can make it NULL.
RegQueryValueEx will execute without filling in the value type.

Listing 3.17 shows an example that uses the default value of the key.
The default value of the key will always be a REG_SZ.

Listing 3.17

```
HKEY hkKey=NULL;

DWORD cbData;
LONG lErrorCode;

LPTSTR  lpszDefaultValue;

// Open a Handle to the Key

if (lErrorCode=RegOpenKeyEx(
HKEY_LOCAL_MACHINE,
"SYSTEM\\CurrentControlSet\\Services\\EventLog
\\Application\\TestApp",
0,
KEY_QUERY_VALUE,
&hkKey)!=ERROR_SUCCESS)
{
// TODO : Add Error Handling Code
}
else
{

// Query the Default Value Size
if (RegQueryValueEx(
hkKey,
NULL,
NULL,
NULL,
NULL,
&cbData
)!=ERROR_SUCCESS)
{
// TODO : Add Error Handling Code
}

lpszDefaultValue = new TCHAR[cbData];
```

```
// Query the Default Value
if (RegQueryValueEx(
hkKey,
NULL,
NULL,
NULL,
(LPBYTE)lpszDefaultValue,
&cbData
)!=ERROR_SUCCESS)
{
// TODO : Add Error Handling Code
}

delete lpszDefaultValue;

RegCloseKey(hkKey);
}
```

Listing 3.18 shows an example of querying the RegQueryValueEx that uses the CString class instead of allocated memory. Notice that even though we use CString, we still have to set the query for the size of the value as well as set the CString buffer.

Listing 3.18

```
HKEY hkKey=NULL;
DWORD cbData;
LONG lErrorCode;
CString csDefaultValue;

// Open a Handle to the Key

if (lErrorCode=RegOpenKeyEx(
HKEY_LOCAL_MACHINE,
"SYSTEM\\CurrentControlSet\\Services\\EventLog
\\Application\\TestApp",
0,
KEY_QUERY_VALUE,
&hkKey)!=ERROR_SUCCESS)
```

```cpp
{
// TODO : Add Error Handling Code
}
else
{

// Query the Default Value Size
if (RegQueryValueEx(
hkKey,
NULL,
NULL,
NULL,
NULL,
&cbData
)!=ERROR_SUCCESS)
{
// TODO : Add Error Handling Code
}

// Query the Default Value Size
if (RegQueryValueEx(
hkKey,
NULL,
NULL,
NULL,
(LPBYTE)csDefaultValue.GetBuffer( cbData ),
&cbData
)!=ERROR_SUCCESS)
{
// TODO : Add Error Handling Code
}

csDefaultValue.ReleaseBuffer();

RegCloseKey(hkKey);

}
```

Traversing the Registry Key

RegEnumKey
RegEnumKeyEx

RegEnumKey and RegEnumKeyEx allow you to traverse the Registry key. They return the name of a subkey of a known parent key based on an integer index to that child. RegEnumKey should be used only with 16-bit applications running under Windows 3.1. RegEnumKeyEx, an extension of RegEnumKey, should be used for 32-bit applications.

RegEnumKey

RegEnumKey has the following four parameters:

1. A handle to an open key or one of the root keys

2. The child key's index

3. A pointer to an allocated memory space

4. The size of the allocated memory space

The first parameter is a handle to an open key or one of the following root keys:

- HKEY_CLASSES_ROOT

- HKEY_CURRENT_USER

- HKEY_LOCAL_MACHINE

- HKEY_USERS

The second parameter is the child key's index expressed as an integer. The first index is 0. Be sure to take into consideration that child keys are not in order by integer index.

The third parameter is a pointer to an allocated memory space that will receive the name of the child key when the parameter returns.

The fourth parameter is the size of the allocated memory space. The key name can be no longer then MAX_PATH + 1.

If RegEnumKey completes successfully, it returns ERROR_SUCCESS; otherwise, it returns an error value. The key being enumerated must have been opened using KEY_ENUMERATE_SUB_KEYS.

The application calling RegEnumKey should start with the index of 0 and continue to call RegEnumKey, incrementing the index until ERROR_NO_MORE_ITEMS is returned. As the application traverses the tree, no changes to the parent key should be made that would effect how the children are indexed. For instance, do not add a child key to the parent key you are traversing.

Listing 3.19 shows an example of traversing a parent.

Listing 3.19

```
HKEY hkKey=NULL;
LONG lErrorCode;
DWORD dwIndex=0;
TCHAR lpName[MAX_PATH+1];
DWORD cbName=MAX_PATH+1;

// Open a Handle to the Key

if (lErrorCode=RegOpenKeyEx(
HKEY_LOCAL_MACHINE,
"SYSTEM\\CurrentControlSet\\Services\\EventLog
\\Application",
0,
KEY_ENUMERATE_SUB_KEYS,
&hkKey)!=ERROR_SUCCESS)
{
// TODO : Add Error Handling Code
}
else
{
  while ((lErrorCode=RegEnumKey(hkKey,dwIndex,lpName,
  cbName))== ERROR_SUCCESS)
  {
    //TODO Do Something the lpName Value
    dwIndex++;
  }
```

```
RegCloseKey(hkKey);
}
```

RegEnumKeyEx

RegEnumKeyEx returns the name of a child key of a known parent key based on an integer index to that child. It also can get the class of the key and find out when it has been last modified. It has the following eight parameters:

1. A handle to an open key or one of the root keys

2. The child key's index

3. A pointer to an allocated memory space that will receive the name of the child key when the parameter returns

4. A pointer to a DWORD

5. Reserved; must be set to NULL

6. A pointer to an allocated memory space that will receive the class name of the child key when the parameter returns

7. A pointer to a DWORD that will hold the size of the allocated memory space for the child key's class name

8. The size; a pointer to a FILETIME structure

The first parameter to RegEnumKeyEx is a handle to an open key or one of the following root keys:

- HKEY_CLASSES_ROOT

- HKEY_CURRENT_USER

- HKEY_LOCAL_MACHINE

- HKEY_USERS

The second parameter is the child key's index expressed as an integer. The first index is 0. Take into consideration that the child keys are not in order by integer index.

The third parameter is a pointer to an allocated memory space that will receive the name of the child key when the parameter returns. It cannot be NULL.

The fourth parameter is a pointer to a DWORD that will hold the size of the allocated memory space for the child key's name. When RegEnumKeyEx returns, the DWORD is set to the size of the child key's name. Unfortunately, you cannot call RegEnumKeyEx with the third parameter as NULL, get the name size from the fourth parameter, allocate the memory, and then recall RegEnumKeyEx to get the child's name. The size does not include the terminating NULL character.

The fifth parameter is reserved; it must be set to NULL.

The sixth parameter is a pointer to an allocated memory space that will receive the class name of the child key when the parameter returns. If you don't want the class name, you can set this parameter to NULL.

The seventh parameter is a pointer to a DWORD that will hold the size of the allocated memory space for the child key's class name. When RegEnumKeyEx returns, the DWORD is set to the size of the child key's class name. Unfortunately, you cannot call RegEnumKeyEx with the seventh parameter set to NULL, get the class name size from the sixth parameter, allocate the memory, and then recall RegEnumKeyEx to get the child's class name. The size does not include the terminating NULL character. If the sixth parameter is NULL, then this parameter can also be NULL.

The eighth parameter is a pointer to a FILETIME structure. Upon the return RegEnumKeyEx, this parameter gets set to the child key's last write time, that is, the last time the child key was modified. The key name can be no longer than MAX_PATH + 1.

If RegEnumKeyEx completes successfully, it returns ERROR_SUCCESS; otherwise, it returns an error value. The key being enumerated must have been opened using KEY_ENUMERATE_SUB_KEYS.

The application that is calling RegEnumKeyEx should start with the index of 0 and continue to call RegEnumKeyEx, incrementing the index until ERROR_NO_MORE_ITEMS is returned. As the application traverses the tree, no changes should be made to the parent key that would effect how the children are indexed. For instance, do not add a child key to the parent key you are traversing.

Listing 3.20 shows an example of the use of RegEnumKeyEx.

Listing 3.20

```
HKEY hkKey=NULL;
LONG lErrorCode;
DWORD dwIndex=0;
TCHAR lpClassName[MAX_CLASSNAME+1];
TCHAR lpName[MAX_KEYNAME+1];
DWORD cbName=MAX_KEYNAME;
DWORD cbClassName=MAX_CLASSNAME;
FILETIME ftTime;

// Open a Handle to the Key

if (lErrorCode=RegOpenKeyEx(
HKEY_LOCAL_MACHINE,
"SYSTEM\\CurrentControlSet\\Services\\EventLog
\\Application",
0,
KEY_ENUMERATE_SUB_KEYS,
&hkKey)!=ERROR_SUCCESS)
{
// TODO : Add Error Handling Code
}
else
{
// Call RegEnumKeyEx, loop while there are more subkeys
while ((lErrorCode=RegEnumKeyEx(hkKey,dwIndex,lpName,
&cbName,NULL,lpClassName,&cbClassName,&ftTime))==
ERROR_SUCCESS)
{

//TODO Do Something the lpName Value and lpClassName Name

// Reset the Sizes
cbName=MAX_KEYNAME;
cbClassName=MAX_CLASSNAME;

dwIndex++;
}
RegCloseKey(hkKey);
}
```

Notice that the maximum size for the class name is set at 100 characters. This setting is arbitrary; RegEnumKeyEx doesn't define the maximum size of the string. However, setting the number of characters to be more than 100 could cause a problem, as the class name would be truncated to 100 characters. You can avoid this by using RegQueryInfoKey to get the maximum class name length of the children in the particular key you are enumerating. We discuss RegQueryInfoKey next.

Getting Information from an Open Key

RegQueryInfoKey

RegQueryInfoKey gets information from an open key. It returns the following:

- Class name associated with the key

- Number of subkeys

- Longest subkey name

- Number of value entries

- Longest value name

- Longest value data length

- Security descriptor

- Last write time

- Longest subkey class name

Information obtained from RegQueryInfoKey can be useful in enumerating keys, since RegQueryInfoKey returns the number of subkeys, the longest subkey name, and the longest subkey class name. The information also can be useful when enumerating values of a key.

RegQueryInfoKey has the following 11 parameters:

1. A handle to an open key or one of the root keys

2. A pointer to an allocated memory space that will be set to the key's class name

3. A pointer to a DWORD that will hold the size of the allocated memory space for the child key's class name

4. Reserved; must be NULL

5. A pointer to a DWORD that receives the number of subkeys within the given key

6. A pointer to a DWORD that receives the longest subkey name

7. A pointer to a DWORD that receives the longest subkey class name

8. A pointer to a DWORD that receives the number of name-value pairs in the key

9. A pointer to a DWORD that receives the longest value name

10. A pointer to a DWORD that receives the length of the security descriptor associated with key

11. A pointer to a FILETIME structure

The first parameter to RegQueryInfoKey is a handle to an open key or one of the following root keys:

- HKEY_CLASSES_ROOT

- HKEY_CURRENT_USER

- HKEY_LOCAL_MACHINE

- HKEY_USERS

The second parameter is a pointer to an allocated memory space that will be set to the class name of the key. If you don't want to retrieve the key's class name, the parameter can be NULL. Because the class name can be any size, the allocated memory space needs to be big enough to handle the key. Try calling RegQueryInfoKey on the parent key of the key for which you want to get the class name. Using the information of the parent's longest subkey class name, you can allocate that amount of memory, since the key for which you are trying to get the class name is a subkey of that parent. The parameter's value does not include the terminating NULL character.

The third parameter is a pointer to a DWORD that will hold the size of the allocated memory space for the child key's class name. When

RegQueryInfoKey returns, the DWORD is set to the size of the child key's class name. Unfortunately, you cannot call RegQueryInfoKey with the seventh parameter set to NULL, get the class name size from the second parameter, allocate the memory, and then recall RegQueryInfoKey to get the child's class name. The size does not include the terminating NULL character. If the second parameter is NULL, then this parameter also can be NULL. The parameter's value does not include the terminating NULL character.

The fourth parameter is reserved; it must be NULL.

The fifth parameter is a pointer to a DWORD. On successful execution of RegQueryInfoKey, this parameter receives the number of subkeys within this given key. If the information is not wanted, the parameter can be NULL.

The sixth parameter is a pointer to a DWORD. On successful execution of RegQueryInfoKey, this parameter receives the longest subkey name. This is useful for allocating memory for the subkey name before calling RegEnumKey or RegEnumKeyEx. The parameter can be NULL if the information is not wanted. The parameter's value does not include the terminating NULL character.

The seventh parameter is a pointer to a DWORD. On successful execution of RegQueryInfoKey, this parameter receives the longest subkey class name. This is useful for allocating memory for the subkey class name before calling RegEnumKeyEx. If the information is not wanted, the parameter can be NULL. The parameter's value does not include the terminating NULL character.

The eighth parameter is a pointer to a DWORD. On successful execution of RegQueryInfoKey, this parameter receives the number of name-value pairs in the key. This is useful for calling RegEnumValue. If the information is not wanted, the parameter can be NULL.

The ninth parameter is a pointer to a DWORD. On successful execution of RegQueryInfoKey, this parameter receives the longest value name. This is useful for allocating memory for the value names when calling RegEnumValue. If the information is not wanted, the parameter can be NULL. The parameter's value does not include the terminating NULL character.

The tenth parameter is a pointer to a DWORD. On successful execution of RegQueryInfoKey, this parameter receives the length of the security descriptor associated with key. If the information is not wanted, the parameter can be NULL.

The eleventh parameter is a pointer to a FILETIME structure. On successful execution of RegQueryInfoKey, the FILETIME structure is set to the key's last write time, that is, the last time the key was written. On a Windows 95 machine, the FILETIME structure attributes will be set to 0, since Windows 95 doesn't keep track of the last write time of a key. If the information is not wanted, the parameter can be NULL.

If RegQueryInfoKey completes successfully, it returns ERROR_SUCCESS; otherwise, it returns an error value. The key being queried must have been opened with KEY_QUERY_VALUE.

Listing 3.21 shows example code that queries all the key information.

Listing 3.21

```
HKEY hkParentKey=NULL;
HKEY hkKey=NULL;
LONG lErrorCode;
DWORD cbParentMaxClassLen;
LPTSTR lpClass;
DWORD cbClass;
DWORD cSubKeys;
DWORD cbMaxSubKeyLen;
DWORD cbMaxClassLen;
DWORD cValues;
DWORD cbMaxValueNameLen;
DWORD cbMaxValueLen;
DWORD cbSecurityDescriptor;
FILETIME ftLastWriteTime;

// Open a Handle to the Parent Key

if (lErrorCode=RegOpenKeyEx(
HKEY_LOCAL_MACHINE,
"SYSTEM\\CurrentControlSet\\Services\\EventLog",
0,
KEY_QUERY_VALUE,
&hkParentKey)!=ERROR_SUCCESS)
{
// TODO : Add Error Handling Code
}
```

```
else
{

if (lErrorCode=RegQueryInfoKey(
hkParentKey,
NULL,
NULL,
NULL,
NULL,
NULL,
&cbParentMaxClassLen,
NULL,
NULL,
NULL,
NULL,
NULL)!=ERROR_SUCCESS)
{
// TODO : Add Error Handling Code
}

RegCloseKey(hkKey);

// Allocate enough Space for the Class Name based on
// the Parents Information

lpClass = new TCHAR[cbParentMaxClassLen+1];

// Open a Handle to the Key

if (lErrorCode=RegOpenKeyEx(
HKEY_LOCAL_MACHINE,
"SYSTEM\\CurrentControlSet\\Services\\EventLog
\\Application",
0,
KEY_QUERY_VALUE,
&hkKey)!=ERROR_SUCCESS)
{
// TODO : Add Error Handling Code
}
```

```
else
{

// Call RegQueryInfoKey

if (lErrorCode=RegQueryInfoKey(
hkKey,
lpClass,
&cbClass,
NULL,
&cSubKeys,
&cbMaxSubKeyLen,
&cbMaxClassLen,
&cValues,
&cbMaxValueNameLen,
&cbMaxValueLen,
&cbSecurityDescriptor,
&ftLastWriteTime)!=ERROR_SUCCESS)
{
// TODO : Add Error Handling Code
}

RegCloseKey(hkKey);
}
delete lpClass;
}
```

Listing 3.22 is a rewrite of Listing 3.20 that illustrates the use of RegQueryInfoKey in enumerating keys.

Listing 3.22

```
HKEY hkKey=NULL;
LONG lErrorCode;
DWORD dwIndex=0;
DWORD iSubKeys;
LPTSTR lpClassName;
LPTSTR lpName;
DWORD cbMaxNameLength;
```

```
DWORD cbMaxClassNameLength;
DWORD cbName;
DWORD cbClassName;
FILETIME  ftTime;

// Open a Handle to the Key

if (lErrorCode=RegOpenKeyEx(
HKEY_LOCAL_MACHINE,
"SYSTEM\\CurrentControlSet\\Services\\EventLog
\\Application",
0,
KEY_QUERY_VALUE,
&hkKey)!=ERROR_SUCCESS)
{
// TODO : Add Error Handling Code
}
else
{

// Call RegQueryInfoKey to get the number of subkeys
// longest subkey name length and longest subkey class
// name length

if (lErrorCode=RegQueryInfoKey(
hkKey,
NULL,
NULL,
NULL,
&iSubKeys,
&cbMaxNameLength,
&cbMaxClassNameLength,
NULL,
NULL,
NULL,
NULL,
NULL)!=ERROR_SUCCESS)
{
```

```
// TODO : Add Error Handling Code
}
else
{

// Allocate enough space

lpName=new TCHAR[cbMaxNameLength+1];
lpClassName=new TCHAR[cbMaxClassNameLength+1];

// Loop Through Subkeys

for (dwIndex=0;dwIndex<iSubKeys;dwIndex++)
{
cbName=cbMaxNameLength;
cbClassName=cbMaxClassNameLength;
RegEnumKeyEx(hkKey,dwIndex,lpName,&cbName,NULL,
lpClassName,&cbClassName,&ftTime);
//TODO Do Something the lpName Value and
//lpClassName Name
}

delete lpName;
delete lpClassName;
}
RegCloseKey(hkKey);
}
```

In Listing 3.20, the code allocated the maximum amount of memory for the subkey name and guessed at the amount of memory of the subkey class. An incorrect guess means the subkey name could be truncated. The rewrite in Listing 3.22 eliminates this problem by using the information supplied from RegQueryInfoKey to allocate the largest amount of memory needed for both strings.

Traversing the Name-Value Pairs

RegEnumValue

RegEnumValue allows you to traverse the name-value pairs in a Registry key. It gets the information based on an integer value index. It has the following eight parameters:

1. A handle to an open key or one of the root keys

2. The value's index

3. An allocated memory space

4. A pointer to a DWORD that will hold the size of the allocated memory space for the name of the name-value pair

5. Reserved; must be set to NULL

6. A pointer to a DWORD that is set to the value type of the particular name-value pair

7. A memory address

8. A pointer to a DWORD that indicates the size of the buffer in the fifth parameter

The first parameter is a handle to an open key or one of the following root keys:

- HKEY_CLASSES_ROOT

- HKEY_CURRENT_USER

- HKEY_LOCAL_MACHINE

- HKEY_USERS

The second parameter is the value's index as an integer. The first index is 0. Take into consideration that name-value pairs are not in order by integer index.

The third parameter is a pointer to an allocated memory space that will receive the name of the name-value pair when the parameter returns. It cannot be NULL.

The fourth parameter is a pointer to a DWORD that will hold the size of the allocated memory space for the name of the name-value pair. When RegEnumValue returns, the DWORD is set to the size of the name of the name-value pair. The size includes the terminating NULL character.

The fifth parameter is reserved; it must be set to NULL.

The sixth parameter is a pointer to a DWORD, which is set to the value type of the particular name-value pair. The type can be any one of the following:

- REG_BINARY

  Binary data in any form

- REG_DWORD

  A 32-bit number

- REG_DWORD_LITTLE_ENDIAN

  A 32-bit number in little-endian format (same as REG_DWORD). In little-endian format, the most significant byte of a word is the high-order word. This is the most common format for computers running Windows NT and Windows 95.

- REG_DWORD_BIG_ENDIAN

  A 32-bit number in big-endian format. In big-endian format, the most significant byte of a word is the low-order word.

- REG_EXPAND_SZ

  A NULL-terminated string that contains unexpanded references to environment variables (for example, "%PATH%"). It will be a Unicode or ANSI string depending on whether you use the Unicode function or ANSI function.

- REG_LINK

  A Unicode symbolic link

- REG_MULTI_SZ

  An array of NULL-terminated strings, terminated by two NULL characters

- REG_NONE

  No defined value type

- REG_RESOURCE_LIST

  A device-driver resource list

- REG_SZ

  A NULL-terminated string. It will be a Unicode or ANSI string,
  depending on whether you use the Unicode function or ANSI function.

The seventh parameter is an address where memory has been allocated
to receive the data being queried.

The eighth parameter is a pointer to a DWORD. When RegEnumValue
is called, the DWORD should indicate the size of the buffer in the fifth parameter. If the value type is REG_SZ, REG_MULTI_SZ, or REG_EXPAND_SZ,
then the DWORD should include the terminating NULL character. When
the function returns, the long value is set to the size of the value, including
the NULL character if the value type is REG_SZ, REG_MULTI_SZ, or
REG_EXPAND_SZ.

If RegEnumValue completes successfully, it returns ERROR_SUCCESS;
otherwise, it returns an error value. The key being queried must have been
opened using KEY_QUERY_VALUE. If you query a value stored under
REG_EXPAND_SZ, the value will not be expanded at the time of the query.
You will need to use a function called ExpandEnvironmentStrings to
expand the value. We do not discuss that function in this book. Index 0 is
always the default value for the key.

Listing 3.23 shows example code using RegEnumValue and
RegQueryInfoKey to view all name-value keys that are of type REG_SZ.

Listing 3.23

```
HKEY hkKey=NULL;
LONG  lErrorCode;
DWORD dwIndex=0;
DWORD cbMaxValueNameLen=0;
LPTSTR  lpName;
DWORD cbName;
DWORD dwType;
```

```
DWORD cbData;
LPTSTR lpszString;

// Open a Handle to the Key

if (lErrorCode=RegOpenKeyEx(
HKEY_LOCAL_MACHINE,
"SYSTEM\\CurrentControlSet\\Services\\EventLog
\\Application\\TestApp",
0,
KEY_QUERY_VALUE,
&hkKey)!=ERROR_SUCCESS)
{
// TODO : Add Error Handling Code
}
else
{

if (lErrorCode=RegQueryInfoKey(
hkKey,
NULL,
NULL,
NULL,
NULL,
NULL,
NULL,
NULL,
&cbMaxValueNameLen,
NULL,
NULL,
NULL)!=ERROR_SUCCESS)
{
// TODO : Add Error Handling Code
}

// Allocated enough room for the Name
lpName = new TCHAR[cbMaxValueNameLen+1];
```

```
// Set Name Size
cbName=cbMaxValueNameLen;

while ((lErrorCode=RegEnumValue(hkKey,dwIndex,lpName,
&cbName,NULL,&dwType,NULL,&cbData))!=ERROR_SUCCESS)
{
// Reset the Size
cbName=cbMaxValueNameLen;

switch (dwType)
{

case REG_SZ :
{
lpszString=new TCHAR[cbData];
lErrorCode=RegEnumValue(hkKey,dwIndex,lpName,&cbName,
NULL,&dwType,(LPBYTE)lpszString,&cbData);

//TODO Do Something with the value

delete lpszString;
break;
}

}

//TODO Do Something the lpName Value and
//lpClassName Name

// Reset the Size
cbName=cbMaxValueNameLen;

dwIndex++;
}

delete lpName;

RegCloseKey(hkKey);
}
```

Deleting a Value in a Key

RegDeleteValue

RegDeleteValue deletes a value in a key. It has the following two parameters:

1. A handle to an open key or one of the root keys

2. The name of the name value pair to delete

The first parameter to RegDeleteValue is a handle to an open key or one of the following root keys:

- HKEY_CLASSES_ROOT

- HKEY_CURRENT_USER

- HKEY_LOCAL_MACHINE

- HKEY_USERS

The second parameter is the name of the name-value pair to delete. If the value is NULL, then the default key value is deleted.

If RegDeleteValue completes successfully, it returns ERROR_SUCCESS; otherwise, it returns an error value. The key being queried must have been opened using KEY_SET_VALUE.

Listing 3.24 shows an example of deleting a value. Before running Listing 3.24, you will need to run Listing 3.7, which creates the value to delete.

Listing 3.24

```
HKEY  hkKey=NULL;
LONG  lErrorCode;

// Open a Handle to the Key
if (lErrorCode=RegOpenKeyEx(
HKEY_LOCAL_MACHINE,
"SYSTEM\\CurrentControlSet\\Services\\EventLog
\\Application\\TestApp",
0,
KEY_SET_VALUE,
```

```
&hkKey)!=ERROR_SUCCESS)
{
// TODO : Add Error Handling Code
}
else
{

if (RegDeleteValue(hkKey,"FooString")!=ERROR_SUCCESS)
{
// TODO : Add Error Handling Code
}

RegCloseKey(hkKey);
}
```

Listing 3.25 shows an example of deleting the default key and then trying to read it.

Listing 3.25
```
HKEY   hkKey=NULL;
LONG   lErrorCode;

// Open a Handle to the Key

if (lErrorCode=RegOpenKeyEx(
HKEY_LOCAL_MACHINE,
"SYSTEM\\CurrentControlSet\\Services\\EventLog
\\Application\\TestApp",
0,
KEY_SET_VALUE,
&hkKey)!=ERROR_SUCCESS)
{
// TODO : Add Error Handling Code
}
else
{

if (lErrorCode=RegDeleteValue(hkKey,NULL)!=ERROR_SUCCESS)
{
```

```
// TODO : Add Error Handling Code
}

RegCloseKey(hkKey);
}
```

Note that when you view the key through regedit.exe, the default value doesn't go away like it does for the other name-value pairs; it just gets set to NULL. NULL can be represented in many ways depending on the regedit.exe you are using.

Copying a Key's Security Descriptor

RegGetKeySecurity

RegGetKeySecurity gets a copy of the security descriptor for a key. It has the following four parameters:

1. A handle to an open key or one of the root keys

2. A SECURITY_INFORMATION structure

3. A pointer to an allocated memory space

4. A pointer to DWORD that indicates the size of the security descriptor

The first parameter is a handle to an open key or one of the following root keys:

- HKEY_CLASSES_ROOT

- HKEY_CURRENT_USER

- HKEY_LOCAL_MACHINE

- HKEY_USERS

The second parameter is a SECURITY_INFORMATION structure that indicates the requested security information. It may be any of the following:

■ OWNER_SECURITY_INFORMATION

Request for the owner identifier of the key

■ GROUP_SECURITY_INFORMATION

Request for the primary group identifier of the key

■ DACL_SECURITY_INFORMATION

Request for the discretionary ACL of the key

■ SACL_SECURITY_INFORMATION

Request for the system ACL of the key

The third parameter is a pointer to an allocated memory space that will contain the security descriptor after RegGetKeySecurity completes successfully.

The fourth parameter is a pointer to a DWORD that indicates the size of the security descriptor. When RegGetKeySecurity returns, the DWORD is set to the size of the security descriptor.

If RegGetKeySecurity completes successfully, it returns ERROR_SUCCESS; otherwise, it returns an error value. The key being queried must have been opened using KEY_READ, KEY_WRITE, KEY_EXECUTE, or KEY_ALL_ACCESS.

Before calling RegGetKeySecurity, you should call RegQueryInfoKey to get the size of the security descriptor.

Listing 3.26 shows an example of RegGetKeySecurity and RegQueryInfoKey. Before running Listing 3.26, you need to run Listing 3.7, which creates the security descriptor.

Listing 3.26

```
HKEY hkKey=NULL;
LONG lErrorCode;
DWORD cbSecurityDescriptor;
PSECURITY_DESCRIPTOR pSecurityDescriptor;

// Open a Handle to the Key

if (lErrorCode=RegOpenKeyEx(
HKEY_LOCAL_MACHINE,
```

```
"SYSTEM\\CurrentControlSet\\Services\\EventLog
\\Application\\TestApp",
0,
KEY_READ | KEY_WRITE | KEY_EXECUTE |KEY_ALL_ACCESS,
&hkKey)!=ERROR_SUCCESS)
{
// TODO : Add Error Handling Code
}
else
{

// Call RegQueryInfoKey to see how much room is needed
// for the Security Descriptor

if (lErrorCode=RegQueryInfoKey(
hkKey,
NULL,
NULL,
NULL,
NULL,
NULL,
NULL,
NULL,
NULL,
NULL,
&cbSecurityDescriptor,
NULL)!=ERROR_SUCCESS)
{
// TODO : Add Error Handling Code
}
else
{

// Allocate room needed for Security Descriptor

pSecurityDescriptor = new BYTE[cbSecurityDescriptor];

// Call RegGetKeySecurity to get the Security Descriptor
```

```
if (lErrorCode=RegGetKeySecurity(
hkKey,
OWNER_SECURITY_INFORMATION,
pSecurityDescriptor,
&cbSecurityDescriptor)!=ERROR_SUCCESS)
{
// TODO : Add Error Handling Code
}

delete pSecurityDescriptor;

}

RegCloseKey(hkKey);
}
```

Setting a Key's Security Descriptor

RegSetSecurityKey

RegSetSecurityKey sets the security descriptor of a key. It has the following three parameters:

1. A handle to an open key or one of the root keys

2. A SECURITY_INFORMATION structure

3. A pointer to a security descriptor

The first parameter is a handle to an open key or one of the following root keys:

- HKEY_CLASSES_ROOT

- HKEY_CURRENT_USER

- HKEY_LOCAL_MACHINE

- HKEY_USERS

The second parameter is a SECURITY_INFORMATION structure that is one of the following:

- OWNER_SECURITY_INFORMATION

  Set for the owner identifier of the key. The process calling RegSetSecurityKey must have WRITE_OWNER permission or have the SE_TAKE_OWNERSHIP_NAME privilege.

- GROUP_SECURITY_INFORMATION

  Set for the primary group identifier of the key. The process calling RegSetSecurityKey must have WRITE_OWNER permission or have the SE_TAKE_OWNERSHIP_NAME privilege.

- DACL_SECURITY_INFORMATION

  Set for the discretionary ACL of the key. The process calling RegSetSecurityKey must have WRITE_DAC permission or be the object's owner.

- SACL_SECURITY_INFORMATION

  Set for the system ACL of the key. The process calling RegSetSecurityKey must have SE_SECURITY_NAME privilege.

The third parameter is a pointer to a security descriptor that the key will obtain.

If RegGetKeySecurity completes successfully, it returns ERROR_SUCCESS; otherwise, it returns an error value. The key being queried must have been opened using KEY_READ, KEY_WRITE, KEY_EXECUTE, or KEY_ALL_ACCESS.

If the first parameter is one of the predefined keys, then it needs to be closed with RegCloseKey so as to save the changes.

Listing 3.27 shows the use of RegGetKeySecurity by limiting the performance data to only interactive users and administrators. This example keeps users with logons to the system from viewing the performance data.

Listing 3.27

```
PSID psidInteractive = NULL;
PSID psidAdmin = NULL;
SID_IDENTIFIER_AUTHORITY siaSID =
```

```
SECURITY_NT_AUTHORITY;
SECURITY_DESCRIPTOR sdSecurityDescriptor;
PACL pDacl = NULL;
DWORD dwAclSize;
HKEY hkKey;
LONG lReturnCode;
BOOL bSuccess = FALSE; // assume this function fails

// Prep Sid with Interactive group
if(!AllocateAndInitializeSid(
&siaSID,
1,
SECURITY_INTERACTIVE_RID,
0, 0, 0, 0, 0, 0, 0,
&psidInteractive
))
{
// TODO : Add Error Handling Code
}


// Prep Sid with admin group
if(!AllocateAndInitializeSid(
&siaSID,
2,
SECURITY_BUILTIN_DOMAIN_RID,
DOMAIN_ALIAS_RID_ADMINS,
0, 0, 0, 0, 0, 0,
&psidAdmin
))
{
// TODO : Add Error Handling Code
}


dwAclSize = sizeof(ACL) +
2 * ( sizeof(ACCESS_ALLOWED_ACE) - sizeof(DWORD) ) +
GetLengthSid(psidInteractive) +
GetLengthSid(psidAdmin) ;
```

```
// Allocate some Memory
pDacl = (PACL)HeapAlloc(GetProcessHeap(), 0,
dwAclSize);
if(pDacl == NULL)
{
// TODO : Add Error Handling Code
}


if(!InitializeAcl(pDacl, dwAclSize, ACL_REVISION))
{
// TODO : Add Error Handling Code
}

// Set the Interactive Access
if(!AddAccessAllowedAce(
pDacl,
ACL_REVISION,
KEY_READ,
psidInteractive
))
{
// TODO : Add Error Handling Code
}


// Set the Administrators Access
if(!AddAccessAllowedAce(
pDacl,
ACL_REVISION,
KEY_ALL_ACCESS,
psidAdmin
))
{
// TODO : Add Error Handling Code
}
```

```
if(!InitializeSecurityDescriptor(&sdSecurityDescriptor,
SECURITY_DESCRIPTOR_REVISION))
{
// TODO : Add Error Handling Code
}


if(!SetSecurityDescriptorDacl(&sdSecurityDescriptor,
TRUE, pDacl, FALSE))
{
// TODO : Add Error Handling Code
}

// Set the Key in the Registry

if (lReturnCode = RegOpenKeyEx(
HKEY_LOCAL_MACHINE,
"SOFTWARE\\Microsoft\\Windows NT\\CurrentVersion\\Perflib",
0,
WRITE_DAC,
&hkKey
)!= ERROR_SUCCESS)
{
// TODO : Add Error Handling Code
}

else
{
if(lReturnCode = RegSetKeySecurity(
hkKey,
(SECURITY_INFORMATION)DACL_SECURITY_INFORMATION,
&sdSecurityDescriptor
)!= ERROR_SUCCESS)
{
// TODO : Add Error Handling Code
}
else
{
```

```
    bSuccess = TRUE;
  }

  RegCloseKey(hkKey);
}

RegCloseKey(HKEY_LOCAL_MACHINE);

//
// free allocated resources
//
if(pDacl != NULL)
HeapFree(GetProcessHeap(), 0, pDacl);

if(psidInteractive != NULL)
FreeSid(psidInteractive);

if(psidAdmin != NULL)
FreeSid(psidAdmin);
```

Using Key Files to Manipulate Keys

RegSaveKey
RegRestoreKey
RegReplaceKey
RegLoadKey
RegUnloadKey

RegSaveKey, RegRestoreKey, RegReplaceKey, RegLoadKey, and RegUnloadKey are used to manipulate keys. Sets of keys—called hives—are stored on the hard disk in a binary file format. Recall from Chapter 1 that a hive is a binary-formatted Registry file that contains a subkey of a major HKEY. There is one hive for each subkey of HKEY_LOCAL_MACHINE and HKEY_USERS. In a file allocation table (FAT) file system, hive files do not have any extensions. Here is a summary of what these APIs do:

- RegSaveKey creates a file in hive format for a specific key. It also creates the key's values and all of its subkeys and their values.

109

- RegRestoreKey restores the file hive back to the Registry.

- RegReplaceKey replaces a whole hive with saved hive files.

- RegLoadKey loads a hive file into a root.

- RegUnloadKey removes the key loaded with RegLoadKey.

RegSaveKey

RegSaveKey creates a file in hive format for a specific key and saves the key and all of its subkeys and values to the file. It can be used to back up the Registry; this is a good idea when writing code to manipulate the Registry. It has the following three parameters:

1. A handle to an open key or one of the root keys

2. A NULL-terminated string that represents the filename

3. A pointer to a SECURITY_ATTRIBUTES attribute structure

The first parameter is a handle to an open key or one of the following root keys:

- HKEY_CLASSES_ROOT

- HKEY_CURRENT_USER

- HKEY_LOCAL_MACHINE

- HKEY_USERS

Note that most keys are not created with the REG_OPTION_ BACKUP_RESTORE option, so the key cannot just be opened. Rather it must be recreated using the REG_OPTION_BACKUP_RESTORE option. Doing this does not change the values, just the key's permissions. Listing 3.28 shows an example of this technique.

The second parameter is a NULL-terminated string that represents the filename. The file cannot already exist.

The third parameter is a pointer to a SECURITY_ATTRIBUTES attribute structure that contains the security attribute for the new file. If the attribute is NULL, then the file gets a default security attribute.

If RegSaveKey completes successfully, it returns ERROR_SUCCESS; otherwise, it returns an error value. The key being queried must have been opened using KEY_QUERY_VALUE.

If the application is being run under Windows NT, then the privileges for the process that call RegSaveKey have to be set to SE_BACKUP_NAME. Listing 3.28 shows an example of the code needed to do this. In Windows 95, privileges are not supported or required, so the additional code can be removed.

Listing 3.28 shows an example of the system hive (created in Listing 3.7) being backed up under Windows NT.

Listing 3.28

```
HKEY hkKey=NULL;
LONG  lErrorCode;

static HANDLE        hToken;
static TOKEN_PRIVILEGES tp;
static LUID          luid;

DWORD dwDisposition;

// Enable backup privilege.

//
// enable backup privilege
//
if(!OpenProcessToken(GetCurrentProcess(),
    TOKEN_ADJUST_PRIVILEGES,
    &hToken ))
{
// TODO : Add Error Handling Code
}

if(!LookupPrivilegeValue(NULL, SE_BACKUP_NAME, &luid))

{
// TODO : Add Error Handling Code
}
```

```
tp.PrivilegeCount       = 1;
tp.Privileges[0].Luid     = luid;
tp.Privileges[0].Attributes = SE_PRIVILEGE_ENABLED;

AdjustTokenPrivileges(hToken, FALSE, &tp,
sizeof(TOKEN_PRIVILEGES),
        NULL, NULL );

if (GetLastError() != ERROR_SUCCESS)
{
// TODO : Add Error Handling Code
}

// Insert your code here to save the Registry
// keys/subkeys.

if (lErrorCode=RegCreateKeyEx(
HKEY_LOCAL_MACHINE,
"SYSTEM",
0,
NULL,
REG_OPTION_BACKUP_RESTORE,
NULL,
NULL,
&hkKey,
&dwDisposition)!=ERROR_SUCCESS)
{
// TODO : Add Error Handling Code
// Disable backup privilege.
AdjustTokenPrivileges( hToken, TRUE, NULL, 0, NULL, NULL);
}
else
{
if
(lErrorCode=RegSaveKey(hkKey,"c:\\temp\\system",NULL)!=
ERROR_SUCCESS)
{
// TODO : Add Error Handling Code
}
```

```
RegCloseKey(hkKey);
}

// Disable backup privilege.

AdjustTokenPrivileges( hToken, TRUE, NULL, 0, NULL, NULL);
```

RegRestoreKey

RegRestoreKey takes the Registry information saved in file by RegSaveKey and writes it over a particular key. It has the following three parameters:

1. A handle to an open key or one of the root keys

2. A NULL-terminated string containing the filename of the keys to restore

3. An option whether to have the key and all the subkeys be volatile

The first parameter to RegRestoreKey is a handle to an open key or one of the following root keys:

- HKEY_CLASSES_ROOT

- HKEY_CURRENT_USER

- HKEY_LOCAL_MACHINE

- HKEY_USERS

Note that most keys were not created with the REG_OPTION_ BACKUP_RESTORE option, so the key cannot just be opened. Rather, it must be recreated with the REG_OPTION_BACKUP_RESTORE option. Doing this does not change the values, just the key's permissions. Listing 3.29 shows an example of this technique.

The second parameter is a NULL-terminated string containing the filename of the keys to restore. If the file was written to a FAT file system, then the file must not have an extension.

The third parameter is an option whether to have the key and all the subkeys be volatile. If a key is restored as volatile, then when the system reboots the old key and its subkeys will return. If a key is restored as nonvolatile, then it becomes permanent. This parameter also can indicate that the whole hive of keys is to be volatile. Following is a summary of the options:

■ REG_OPTION_NON_VOLATILE replaces the subkeys and the values with the subkeys and values in the file.

■ REG_OPTION_VOLATILE replaces the subkeys and values with a volatile (temporary) set of subkeys and values.

■ REG_WHOLE_HIVE_VOLATILE restores the whole hive as volatile and replaces the given key as volatile with the attributes of the file indicated in the second parameter.

If the application is running under Windows NT, then the privileges for the process that call RegRestoreKey have to be set to SE_RESTORE_NAME. Listing 3.29 is an example of the code needed to do this. Use Listing 3.28 to create the system file that is used in Listing 3.29.

In Windows 95, privileges are not supported or required, so the additional code can be removed.

If RegRestoreKey completes successfully, then it returns ERROR_SUCCESS; otherwise, it returns an error value.

Listing 3.29

```
HKEY hkKey=NULL;
LONG  lErrorCode;

static HANDLE hToken;
static TOKEN_PRIVILEGES tp;
static LUID luid;

DWORD dwDisposition;

// Enable backup privilege.
```

```
//
// enable backup privilege
//
if(!OpenProcessToken(GetCurrentProcess(),
    TOKEN_ADJUST_PRIVILEGES,
    &hToken ))
{
// TODO : Add Error Handling Code
}

if(!LookupPrivilegeValue(NULL, SE_RESTORE_NAME, &luid))

{
// TODO : Add Error Handling Code
}

tp.PrivilegeCount       = 1;
tp.Privileges[0].Luid    = luid;
tp.Privileges[0].Attributes = SE_PRIVILEGE_ENABLED;

AdjustTokenPrivileges(hToken, FALSE, &tp,
sizeof(TOKEN_PRIVILEGES),
        NULL, NULL );

if (GetLastError() != ERROR_SUCCESS)
{
// TODO : Add Error Handling Code
}

// Insert your code here to save the Registry
// keys/subkeys.

if (lErrorCode=RegCreateKeyEx(
HKEY_LOCAL_MACHINE,
"SYSTEM ",
0,
NULL,
REG_OPTION_BACKUP_RESTORE,
```

```
NULL,
NULL,
&hkKey,
&dwDisposition)!=ERROR_SUCCESS)
{
// TODO : Add Error Handling Code
// Disable backup privilege.
AdjustTokenPrivileges( hToken, TRUE, NULL, 0, NULL, NULL);
}
else
{
if (lErrorCode=RegRestoreKey(hkKey,"c:\\temp\\system",
REG_WHOLE_HIVE_VOLATILE)!=ERROR_SUCCESS)
{
// TODO : Add Error Handling Code
}

RegCloseKey(hkKey);
}

// Disable backup privilege.

AdjustTokenPrivileges( hToken, TRUE, NULL, 0, NULL, NULL);
```

RegLoadKey

RegLoadKey loads a hive saved with RegSaveKey into either one of these roots HKEY_LOCAL_MACHINE or HKEY_USERS. The default roots are really keys under these roots. You cannot use RegLoadKey to load a hive into HKEY_CLASSES_ROOT or HKEY_CURRENT_USER.

RegLoadKey has the following three parameters:

1. An open key handle

2. A NULL-terminated string that contains the name of the subkey under which you want to create the hive

3. A NULL-terminated string that contains the name of the file in which you saved the hive

The first parameter is an open key handle returned from RegConnectRegistry or one of these root keys:

- HKEY_LOCAL_MACHINE

- HKEY_USERS

The second parameter is a NULL-terminated string that contains the name of the subkey under which you want to create the hive.

The third parameter is a NULL-terminated string that contains the name of the file under which you saved the hive using RegLoadKey. A hive is a descendant of HKEY_LOCAL_MACHINE or HKEY_USERS and must have been saved by RegLoadKey. If the file was written to a FAT file system, then the file must not have an extension. If the first parameter is an open key from RegConnectRegistry, then the filename is relative to the remote computer.

If the application is being run under Windows NT, then the privileges for the process that call RegLoadKey must be set to SE_RESTORE_NAME. Listing 3.30 is an example of the code needed to do this. Use Listing 3.28 to create the system file that is used in example 3.30.

In Windows 95, privileges are not supported or required, so the additional code can be removed.

The key created is volatile, so it is gone the next time the system reboots. If RegLoadKey completes successfully, it returns ERROR_SUCCESS; otherwise, it returns an error value.

Listing 3.30

```
HKEY hkKey=NULL;
LONG  lErrorCode;

static HANDLE      hToken;
static TOKEN_PRIVILEGES tp;
static LUID        luid;

// Enable backup privilege.

//
// enable backup privilege
//
```

```
if(!OpenProcessToken(GetCurrentProcess(),
    TOKEN_ADJUST_PRIVILEGES,
    &hToken ))
{
// TODO : Add Error Handling Code
}

if(!LookupPrivilegeValue(NULL, SE_RESTORE_NAME, &luid))

{
// TODO : Add Error Handling Code
}

tp.PrivilegeCount = 1;
tp.Privileges[0].Luid = luid;
tp.Privileges[0].Attributes = SE_PRIVILEGE_ENABLED;

AdjustTokenPrivileges(hToken, FALSE, &tp,
sizeof(TOKEN_PRIVILEGES), NULL, NULL );

if (GetLastError() != ERROR_SUCCESS)
{
// TODO : Add Error Handling Code
}

if (lErrorCode=RegLoadKey(HKEY_LOCAL_MACHINE,"SYSTEM2",
"c:\\temp\\system")!=ERROR_SUCCESS)
{
// TODO : Add Error Handling Code
}

// Disable backup privilege.

AdjustTokenPrivileges( hToken, TRUE, NULL, 0, NULL, NULL);
```

RegUnLoadKey

RegUnLoadKey unloads the key, its values, and its subkeys and their values from the Registry; it undoes what RegLoadKey does. It has the following two parameters:

1. An open key handle returned from RegConnectRegistry or one of the root keys

2. A NULL-terminated string that contains the name of the subkey under which you want to create the hive

The first parameter is an open key handle returned from RegConnectRegistry or one of these root keys:

- HKEY_LOCAL_MACHINE

- HKEY_USERS

The second parameter is a NULL-terminated string that contains the name of the subkey under which you want to create the hive.

The files specified in RegLoadKey to create this Registry key are not affected by this API. If RegUnLoadKey completes successfully, it returns ERROR_SUCCESS; otherwise, it returns an error value.

If the application is running under Windows NT, then the privileges for the process that calls RegUnLoadKey must be set to SE_RESTORE_NAME. Listing 3.31 is an example of the code needed to do this. Make sure you run Listing 3.30 before running Listing 3.31 as doing this ensures there is a key to unload.

In Windows 95, privileges are not supported or required, so the additional code can be removed.

Listing 3.31

```
HKEY hkKey=NULL;
LONG lErrorCode;

static HANDLE          hToken;
static TOKEN_PRIVILEGES tp;
static LUID            luid;
```

```
// Enable backup privilege.

//
// enable backup privilege
//
if(!OpenProcessToken(GetCurrentProcess(),
TOKEN_ADJUST_PRIVILEGES,
&hToken ))
{
// TODO : Add Error Handling Code
}

if(!LookupPrivilegeValue(NULL, SE_RESTORE_NAME, &luid))

{
// TODO : Add Error Handling Code
}

tp.PrivilegeCount       = 1;
tp.Privileges[0].Luid    = luid;
tp.Privileges[0].Attributes = SE_PRIVILEGE_ENABLED;

AdjustTokenPrivileges(hToken, FALSE, &tp,
sizeof(TOKEN_PRIVILEGES),NULL, NULL );

if (GetLastError() != ERROR_SUCCESS)
{
// TODO : Add Error Handling Code
}

if (lErrorCode=RegUnLoadKey(HKEY_LOCAL_MACHINE,"SYSTEM2")
!=ERROR_SUCCESS)
{
// TODO : Add Error Handling Code
}

// Disable backup privilege.
```

```
RegCloseKey(HKEY_LOCAL_MACHINE);

AdjustTokenPrivileges( hToken, TRUE, NULL, 0, NULL, NULL);
```

Notice that Listing 3.31 calls RegCloseKey on HKEY_LOCAL_MACHINE before exiting to ensure that the changes affect the Registry right away and the results can be seen with regedit.exe.

RegReplaceKey

RegReplaceKey replaces a hive with a saved hive created by RegSaveKey. The replacement occurs only when the system is rebooted. This is a good technique for installing software that affects system components that are in use when the software is installing. For instance, if the software needs a Registry key to install but must change the key to have the installation complete, the application could use a combination of RegSaveKey, RegReplaceKey, and RegLoadKey.

RegReplaceKey has the following four parameters:

1. An open key handle returned from RegConnectRegistry or one of the root keys

2. A subkey of the first parameter that represents a hive

3. A NULL-terminated string that points to the hive to load when the system is restarted

4. A NULL-terminated string that points to a file that receives a backup of the hive

The first parameter is an open key handle returned from RegConnectRegistry or one of the following root keys:

- HKEY_LOCAL_MACHINE

- HKEY_USERS

- HKEY_CLASSES_ROOT

- HKEY_CURRENT_USER

The second parameter is a subkey of the first parameter that represents a hive. If the first parameter is HKEY_CLASSES_ROOT or HKEY_CURRENT_USER, then the second parameter can be NULL.

The third parameter is a NULL-terminated string that points to the hive to load when the system is restarted. If the file was written to a FAT file system, then the file must not have an extension. If the first parameter is an open key from RegConnectRegistry, then the filename is relative to the remote computer.

The fourth parameter is a NULL-terminated string that points to a file that receives a backup of the hive. If the file was written to a FAT file system, then the file must not have an extension. If the first parameter is an open key from RegConnectRegistry, then the filename is relative to the remote computer.

If the application is being run under Windows NT, then the privileges for the process that calls RegReplaceKey have to be set to SE_RESTORE_NAME. Listing 3.32 is an example of the code needed to do this. Use Listing 3.30 to create the system file that is used in Listing 3.32.

In Windows 95, privileges are not supported or required, so the additional code can be removed.

If RegReplaceKey completes successfully, it returns ERROR_SUCCESS; otherwise, it returns an error value.

Warning: Running Listing 3.32 is extremely dangerous; at worst, you may have to reinstall your operating system and all the programs on it. If things do go wrong and you are running a FAT file system and you can boot to DOS instead of going to Windows NT or Windows 95, then there might be a fix. When RegSaveKey is executed in Listing 3.29, a file is created in the temp directory called "system." When RegReplaceKey is executed in Listing 3.32, the system file from the temp directory is copied to c:\winnt\system32\config\system. Two backups are made of data that was in c:\winnt\system32\config\system. One is called "backup" and is stored in c:\temp; this is the one your application created with RegReplaceKey. The second one is called c:\winnt\system32\config\system.alt. It also is created when RegReplaceKey is called. If something goes wrong and Windows will not boot, go into DOS and copy one of the backups to c:\winnt\system32\config\system.

Listing 3.32

```
HKEY hkKey=NULL;
 [0].Luid    = luid;
tp.Privileges[0].Attributes = SE_PRIVILEGE_ENABLED;

AdjustTokenPrivileges(hToken, FALSE, &tp,
sizeof(TOKEN_PRIVILEGES),
        NULL, NULL );

if (GetLastError() != ERROR_SUCCESS)
{
// TODO : Add Error Handling Code
}

if (lErrorCode=RegReplaceKey(HKEY_LOCAL_MACHINE,
"SYSTEM","c:\\temp\\system","c:\\temp\\backup")
!=ERROR_SUCCESS)
{
// TODO : Add Error Handling Code
}

// Disable backup privilege.

AdjustTokenPrivileges( hToken, TRUE, NULL, 0, NULL, NULL);
```

Getting Multiple Values from a Key

RegQueryMultipleValues

RegQueryMultipleValues allows an application to get multiple values from a key. Each name-value pair to be queried must be a separate VALENT structure. An array of VALENT structures are created and passed to RegQueryMultipleValues. The API then fills in the array with pointers to a buffer in which the value data resides.

RegQueryMultipleValues has the following four parameters:

1. A handle to a key you opened or one of the root keys

2. An address to an array of VALENT structures

3. An address to an allocated buffer

4. A pointer to a DWORD

The first parameter is either a handle to a key you opened by calling RegOpenKey, RegOpenKeyEx, RegCreateKey, RegCreateKeyEx, or RegConnectRegistry or one of the following root keys:

- HKEY_CLASSES_ROOT

- HKEY_CURRENT_USER

- HKEY_LOCAL_MACHINE

- HKEY_USERS

The second parameter is an address to an array of VALENT structures.

The third parameter is an address to an allocated buffer. The buffer will hold the value data when RegQueryMultipleValues returns.

The fourth parameter is a pointer to a DWORD. When RegQueryMultipleValues is called, the DWORD is set to the size of the buffer. When it returns, the DWORD is set to the size of the value data for all the values in the VALENT array.

If RegQueryMultipleValues completes successfully, it returns ERROR_SUCCESS; otherwise, it returns an error value.

Listing 3.33 shows an example that uses RegQueryMultipleValues. It is a rewrite of Listing 3.15, which does exactly the same thing. Before running Listing 3.33, you need to run Listing 3.7, which creates the name-value pairs to query.

Listing 3.33

```
HKEY hkKey=NULL;
LONG lErrorCode;
LPTSTR lpValueBuf=NULL;
DWORD dwTotsize=1000;
VALENT pvalArray[5];
DWORD cbMaxValueLen;

// Open a Handle to the Key
```

```
if (lErrorCode=RegOpenKeyEx(
HKEY_LOCAL_MACHINE,
"SYSTEM\\CurrentControlSet\\Services\\EventLog
\\Application\\TestApp",
0,
KEY_QUERY_VALUE,
&hkKey)!=ERROR_SUCCESS)
{
// TODO : Add Error Handling Code
}
else
{

// Query the Default Value

pvalArray[0].ve_valuename=NULL;
pvalArray[0].ve_valuelen=0;
pvalArray[0].ve_valueptr=0;
pvalArray[0].ve_type=REG_SZ;

// Query FooString which is a REG_SZ

pvalArray[1].ve_valuename=NULL;
pvalArray[1].ve_valuename =
new TCHAR[_tcslen("FooString")+1];
_tcscpy(pvalArray[1].ve_valuename,"FooString");
pvalArray[1].ve_valuelen=0;
pvalArray[1].ve_valueptr=0;
pvalArray[1].ve_type=REG_SZ;

// Query FooPath which is a REG_EXPAND_SZ

pvalArray[2].ve_valuename=NULL;
pvalArray[2].ve_valuename =
new TCHAR[_tcslen("FooPath")+1];
_tcscpy(pvalArray[2].ve_valuename,"FooPath");
pvalArray[2].ve_valuelen=0;
pvalArray[2].ve_valueptr=0;
pvalArray[2].ve_type=REG_EXPAND_SZ;
```

```
// Query FooDWORD which is a REG_DWORD

pvalArray[3].ve_valuename=NULL;
pvalArray[3].ve_valuename = new
TCHAR[_tcslen("FooDWORD")+1];
_tcscpy(pvalArray[3].ve_valuename,"FooDWORD");
pvalArray[3].ve_valuelen=0;
pvalArray[3].ve_valueptr=0;
pvalArray[3].ve_type=REG_DWORD;

// Query FooDWORD which is a REG_MULTI_SZ

pvalArray[4].ve_valuename=NULL;
pvalArray[4].ve_valuename = new
TCHAR[_tcslen("FooStrings")+1];
_tcscpy(pvalArray[4].ve_valuename,"FooStrings");
pvalArray[4].ve_valuelen=0;
pvalArray[4].ve_valueptr=0;
pvalArray[4].ve_type=REG_MULTI_SZ;

// Call RegQueryMultipleValues Once to get the Size
// of the buffer

if (lErrorCode=RegQueryInfoKey(
hkKey,
NULL,
NULL,
NULL,
NULL,
NULL,
NULL,
NULL,
NULL,
&cbMaxValueLen,
NULL,
NULL)!=ERROR_SUCCESS)
{
// TODO : Add Error Handling Code
}
```

```
else
{
dwTotsize=cbMaxValueLen*5;
// Allocate some memory

lpValueBuf= new TCHAR[dwTotsize];

// Call Again to fill in the Buffer;

if (lErrorCode=RegQueryMultipleValues(
hkKey,
pvalArray,
5,
lpValueBuf,
&dwTotsize
)!=ERROR_SUCCESS)
{
// TODO : Add Error Handling Code
}

delete lpValueBuf;
}

delete pvalArray[1].ve_valuename;
delete pvalArray[2].ve_valuename;
delete pvalArray[3].ve_valuename;
delete pvalArray[4].ve_valuename;


RegCloseKey(hkKey);
}
```

Notifying an Application That a Key Has Changed

RegNotifyChangeKeyValue

RegNotifyChangeKeyValue signals an event when a key has changed. It can be used one of two ways. Either it signals an event when the key is changed, or it is called and will not return until the key has changed. If the first approach is taken, then the application must implement the event handle to process the event.

RegNotifyChangeKeyValue has the following five parameters:

1. A handle to an open key or one of the root keys

2. A bool

3. A DWORD that filters out the type of changes to be watched for

4. The event that is to be signaled if the event-handling option is to be used

5. A bool that signals how RegNotifyChangeKeyValue will be used

The first parameter is a handle to an open key or one of the following root keys:

■ HKEY_CLASSES_ROOT

■ HKEY_CURRENT_USER

■ HKEY_LOCAL_MACHINE

■ HKEY_USERS

The second parameter is a bool. If the parameter is set to TRUE, both the key and all of its subkeys are watched for changes. If the parameter is set to FALSE , then only key changes are watched for.

The third parameter is a DWORD. This parameter filters out the type of changes to be watched for. The filters can be combined with a bitwise OR or a pipe |. The filters can be one of the following:

■ REG_NOTIFY_CHANGE_NAME

Changes to key names or creations and deletions of a key

- REG_NOTIFY_CHANGE_ATTRIBUTES

  Attribute changes to a key

- REG_NOTIFY_CHANGE_LAST_SET

  Changes to the last write time of a key

- REG_NOTIFY_CHANGE_SECURITY

  Security descriptor changes to a key

The fourth parameter is the event that is to be signaled if the event-handling option is to be used. If this option is not going to be used, then this parameter can be NULL and the fifth parameter must be FALSE.

The fifth parameter is a bool that signals whether RegNotifyChangeKeyValue is going to be used to trigger event handling (TRUE) or is going to loop until a change occurs (FALSE).

RegNotifyChangeKeyValue doesn't work with remote handles that are opened using RegConnectRegistry.

If RegQueryMultipleValues completes successfully, it returns ERROR_SUCCESS; otherwise, it returns an error value.

Listing 3.34 shows an example of using RegNotifyChangeKeyValue. Before running Listing 3.34, you need to run Listing 3.7, which creates the name-value pairs to query. While RegQueryMultipleValues is waiting for an event, use regedit.exe to create a key in the TestApp key. The listing will then exit.

Listing 3.34

```
HKEY hkKey=NULL;
LONG lErrorCode;

// Open a Handle to the Key

if (lErrorCode=RegOpenKeyEx(
HKEY_LOCAL_MACHINE,
"SYSTEM\\CurrentControlSet\\Services\\EventLog
\\Application\\TestApp",
0,
KEY_ALL_ACCESS,
&hkKey)!=ERROR_SUCCESS)
```

```
{
// TODO : Add Error Handling Code
}
else
{
if (lErrorCode=RegNotifyChangeKeyValue(
hkKey,
TRUE,
REG_NOTIFY_CHANGE_NAME | REG_NOTIFY_CHANGE_ATTRIBUTES,
NULL,
FALSE
)!=ERROR_SUCCESS)
{
// TODO : Add Error Handling Code
}

RegCloseKey(hkKey);
}
```

Chapter 4

Using the Registry APIs in Visual Basic Applications

The Registry APIs provided by the Win32 API (specifically the advapi32.dll dynamic link library) also can be used in your Visual Basic applications. In Chapters 1–3, we described how to use the Registry APIs in C/C++ applications. In this chapter, we describe the steps you should consider taking when utilizing the Registry from within a Visual Basic application.

We begin with a brief overview of the Registry. In this way, Visual Basic developers need not read through the first three chapters before they can start writing programs using the Registry API. And if you are already familiar with the Registry, you can skip the overview section and jump right into the examples.

The examples illustrate the use of many of the Registry APIs, including RegCreateKeyEx, RegOpenKeyEx, RegSetValueEx, RegConnectRegistry, RegQueryValueEx, RegEnumValue, RegEnumKeyEx, RegDeleteKey, and RegCloseKey. The value types used within the examples are REG_SZ, REG_DWORD, REG_EXPAND_SZ, and REG_MULTI_SZ.

Overview of the Registry and the Registry APIs

The Registry is a centralized database used by applications and system components to store and retrieve configuration and initialization data. The Registry information can be manually inserted into the Registry via Registry tools such as regedt32.exe in Windows NT 3.51 and regedit.exe in Windows NT 4.0 and Windows 95. The information also can be written to the Registry

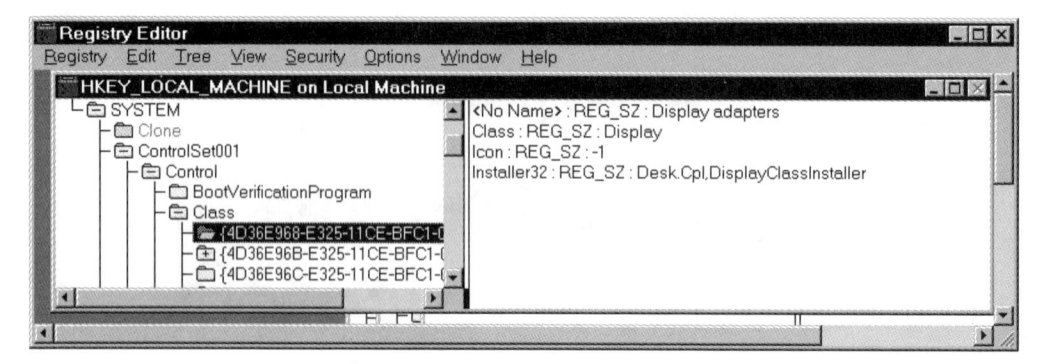

Figure 4.1 <NO NAME> in regedt32.exe

by importing a registration file. Further, Win32 provides a set of APIs to programmatically access the Registry.

The Registry is stored as a tree structured as a hierarchy. Each node in the tree is a key. Each key can have zero to many name-value pairs. Each name-value pair has three components: value name, value type, and value data. The value name is optional. If there is no value name, then <NO NAME> is displayed when the name-value pair is viewed with the Registry tool regedt32.exe. Figure 4.1 shows how the <NO NAME> value appears when viewed with the regedt32.exe tool.

In the figure, value data Display Adapters does not have a value name, while other values all have names, such as Class and Icon. The <NO NAME> value can be created by using the 16-bit function RegSetValue, if necessary.

In 16-bit applications, the name-value pairs do not have names because the value name concept does not exist in 16-bit applications. That is, only one name-value pair without a name can be associated with a single key. None of the 16-bit Registry APIs for setting and retrieving value information have a value name parameter. For instance, the 32-bit RegSetValueEx function must provide a specific value name and its associated data, while the 16-bit RegSetValue function needs to provide only the value data. The *Ex* in RegSetValueEx indicates that the function is a 32-bit version of the function. However, not all Registry functions that omit Ex in the name are automatically 16-bit functions.

Each value includes, in addition to the value name, the type of the value data. The data is stored based on the value type. Commonly used value types are as follows:

- REG_SZ, which specifies a Unicode NULL-terminated string

- REG_DWORD, which stores a 32-bit number

- REG_BINARY, which specifies that the data is a free-form binary

- REG_MULTI_SZ, which specifies the value data to include multiple Unicode strings

Note: Unicode characters contain 2 bytes to represent the character code, while ANSI contains only 1 byte to represent the character code.

A special format is used to specify multiple strings within the value data. Each string must end with a NULL character.

A key must be opened before any name-value pair within the key can be manipulated. When a key is opened, a handle is returned for the open key. This handle is used in all subsequent calls to manipulate the name-value pairs within the key.

There are two ways to open a key: invoke either the RegCreateKeyEx/ RegCreateKey function or the RegOpenKeyEx/RegOpenKey function. Invoking RegCreateKeyEx/RegCreateKey creates the key if it doesn't already exist and then returns the handle to the key. If the key already exists, the last parameter for RegCreateKeyEx will return REG_OPENED_ EXISTING_KEY so that you can test for which operation occurred; that is, the key was either opened or created and then opened. Invoking the RegOpenKeyEx/RegOpenKey function results in a return of the key handle if the key exists.

Every key handle returned by RegCreateKeyEx or RegOpenKeyEx is a system resource. When an application has finished using the open Registry key, it should close the key by calling the function RegCloseKey.

To delete a key, use the RegDeleteKey function. RegDeleteKey also will delete all the values associated within the specified key. In an NT environment, however, if the key contains subkeys the specified key will not be deleted.

Certain keys are always opened by the operating system. These keys, which have reserved handles, are predefined and are as follows:

- **HKEY_LOCAL_MACHINE**. Contains configuration information particular to a computer. Its name can be confusing because it implies that this key is on the local machine. However, when you connect to the Registry on a remote machine, that Registry will also have an HKEY_LOCAL_MACHINE key for that particular remote machine.

- **HKEY_CLASSES_ROOT.** Accessed by Windows shell applications and OLE applications. This key contains the same information as HKEY_LOCAL_MACHINE\Software.

- **HKEY_USERS.** Stores user profiles on the local machine.

- **HKEY_CURRENT_USER.** A subkey of HKEY_USERS.

- **HKEY_CURRENT_CONFIG.** Contains the hardware profile for the system startup.

- **HKEY_DYN_DATA.** Contains performance data.

Values within an open key can be created, queried, modified, and deleted. To create a value within the open key, use the RegSetValueEx or RegSetValue function as described earlier in the chapter. RegSetValueEx can set multiple values within the key, but RegSetValue can set only one value for the key, since the value does not have a name and only one value without a name is allowed. When calling RegSetValueEx, you must include parameters such as the key handle, the value name, the value type, and the value data.

Value information can be queried by calling the RegQueryValueEx or RegQueryValue function. RegQueryValue retrieves only the value data associated with a key, since there is only a value and no name associated with a key in the 16-bit environment.

A named value can be deleted by calling the RegDeleteValue function. If no value name is provided, the value set by RegSetValue will be deleted.

All values associated with a specified key, including name, type, and data, can be enumerated by calling the RegEnumValueEx function.

Registry API Declarations in Visual Basic

Visual Basic provides functions such as DeleteSetting, GetSetting, GetAllSettings, and SaveSetting to retrieve the Registry information. But these functions access only the Registry entries within HKEY_CURRENT_USER\SOFTWARE\VB and VBA program settings. All other Registry manipulation, including reading from and writing to the Registry, must use the Registry functions from the Win32 API.

A Visual Basic application must make some declarations before it can use the Register APIs. First, the application source must declare the prototypes for the Registry functions the application will use. The prototypes must be compatible with the C Registry functions that are exported by advapi32.dll. Then, the application source must define compatible declarations for the structures and constants used when calling the Registry API.

The Registry function prototypes, constants, types, and data structure definitions can be found in winreg.h, which is provided with Visual C++ 4.x. The predefined value type definitions such as REG_DWORD and REG_SZ also can be found in winnt.h in Visual C++ 4.x. These definitions can be found in earlier versions of Visual C++ such as Visual C++ 2.x.

Besides the Registry API definitions provided by Visual C++, Visual Basic itself provides a file called Win32api.txt that contains all the constants, types, and declare statements for Win32 APIs, including those that must be declared in Visual Basic's standard module. A standard module is a module that contains only declare statements, types, and data declarations and definitions. Win32api.txt is in Visual Basic's \winapi directory when Visual Basic is installed on your machine.

Listing 4.1 defines all the reserved key handles defined by the system. Among these handles, HKEY_CURRENT_CONFIG and HKEY_DYN_DATA are available only under Windows NT 4.0 or later versions. The const statement in Listing 4.1 declares a name for use with each literal value.

Listing 4.1

```
Public Const HKEY_CLASSES_ROOT = &H80000000
Public Const HKEY_CURRENT_USER = &H80000001
Public Const HKEY_LOCAL_MACHINE = &H80000002
Public Const HKEY_USERS = &H80000003
Public Const HKEY_PERFORMANCE_DATA = &H80000004
Public Const HKEY_CURRENT_CONFIG = &H80000005
Public Const HKEY_DYN_DATA = &H80000006
```

Listing 4.2 enumerates all the Registry value type constants, along with a description for each.

Listing 4.3 enumerates all the options for a key creation type value.

Listing 4.2

```
Public Const REG_NONE = 0              ' No value type
Public Const REG_SZ = 1                ' Unicode nul
                                       ' terminated string
Public Const REG_EXPAND_SZ = 2         ' Unicode nul
                                       ' terminated string
Public Const REG_BINARY = 3            ' Free form binary
Public Const REG_DWORD = 4             ' 32-bit number
Public Const REG_DWORD_LITTLE_ENDIAN = 4 ' 32-bit number
                                  ' (same as REG_DWORD)
Public Const REG_DWORD_BIG_ENDIAN = 5  ' 32-bit number
Public Const REG_LINK = 6              ' Symbolic Link
                                       ' (unicode)
Public Const REG_MULTI_SZ = 7          ' Multiple Unicode
                                       ' strings
Public Const REG_RESOURCE_LIST = 8     ' Resource list in
                                       ' the resource map
Public Const REG_FULL_RESOURCE_DESCRIPTOR = 9 ' Resource
                  ' list in the hardware description
Public Const REG_RESOURCE_REQUIREMENTS_LIST = 10
```

Listing 4.3

```
' Reg Create Type Values...
Global Const REG_OPTION_RESERVED = 0       ' Parameter
                                           ' is reserved
Global Const REG_OPTION_NON_VOLATILE = 0 ' Key is
                    ' preserved when system is rebooted
Global Const REG_OPTION_VOLATILE = 1       ' Key is not
                    ' preserved when system is rebooted
Global Const REG_OPTION_CREATE_LINK = 2    ' Created key
                                ' is a symbolic link
Global Const REG_OPTION_BACKUP_RESTORE = 4  ' open for
                                ' backup or restore
```

In Listing 4.3, the REG_OPTION_NON_VOLATILE and REG_OPTION_VOLATILE options will be used in RegCreateKeyEx to specify a special option for the key. VOLATILE in the listing means the key is only kept in memory; it will not be preserved when the system is restarted. A volatile key cannot be saved to permanent storage; that is, a volatile key cannot be saved by RegSaveKey. In Windows NT, a key can be volatile. However, in Windows 95 if a special option for a key is defined as REG_OPTION_ VOLATILE, a key can still be saved by calling RegSaveKey.

Listing 4.4 enumerates all the security options allowed on a key. In the listing, &H is used to represent hexadecimal numbers by preceding the number in the proper range. For example, &H11 represents decimal 17 in hexadecimal notation. & is a type-definition character; it represents data type long.

Listing 4.4

```
' Reg Key Security Options
Public Const READ_CONTROL = &H20000
Public Const KEY_QUERY_VALUE = &H1
Public Const KEY_SET_VALUE = &H2
Public Const KEY_CREATE_SUB_KEY = &H4
Public Const KEY_ENUMERATE_SUB_KEYS = &H8
Public Const KEY_NOTIFY = &H10
Public Const KEY_CREATE_LINK = &H20
Public Const KEY_READ = ((STANDARD_RIGHTS_READ Or
KEY_QUERY_VALUE Or KEY_ENUMERATE_SUB_KEYS Or
KEY_NOTIFY) And (Not SYNCHRONIZE))
Public Const KEY_WRITE = ((STANDARD_RIGHTS_WRITE Or
KEY_SET_VALUE Or KEY_CREATE_SUB_KEY) And
(Not SYNCHRONIZE))
Public Const KEY_EXECUTE = (KEY_READ)
Public Const KEY_ALL_ACCESS = ((STANDARD_RIGHTS_ALL Or
KEY_QUERY_VALUE Or KEY_SET_VALUE Or KEY_CREATE_SUB_KEY
Or KEY_ENUMERATE_SUB_KEYS Or KEY_NOTIFY Or
KEY_CREATE_LINK) And (Not SYNCHRONIZE))
Public Const STANDARD_RIGHTS_READ = (READ_CONTROL)
Public Const STANDARD_RIGHTS_WRITE = (READ_CONTROL)
Public Const KEY_EXECUTE = ((KEY_READ) And
(Not SYNCHRONIZE))
```

The security information provided in this listing is used to specify the security access mask for a Registry key. The access mask contains 4 bytes and is defined as follows:

```
typedef struct _ACCESS_MASK {
WORD    SpecificRights;
BYTE    StandardRights;
BYTE    AccessSystemAcl : 1;
BYTE    Reserved : 3;
BYTE    GenericAll : 1;
BYTE    GenericExecute : 1;
BYTE    GenericWrite : 1;
BYTE    GenericRead : 1;
} ACCESS_MASK;
```

Listing 4.5 shows two of the Win32 Registry API return codes.

Listing 4.5

```
#define ERROR_SUCCESS               0&
#define ERROR_NO_MORE_ITEMS         259&
```

Return code ERROR_SUCCESS means the function was successfully performed. ERROR_NO_MORE_ITEMS is returned from RegEnumValue to indicate that all the values have been enumerated. For a complete list of the return codes of the registry APIs, refer to winerror.h, which is provided by Visual C++ 4.x.

Listing 4.6 shows the Registry function RegConnectRegistry prototype declaration for use within Visual Basic.

Listing 4.6

```
Declare Function RegConnectRegistry Lib
"advapi32.dll" Alias "RegConnectRegistryA"
(ByVal lpMachineName As String, ByVal hKey As Long,
phkResult As Long) As Long
```

The RegConnectRegistry function defined in Listing 4.6 also can be defined as follows:

```
Declare Function RegConnectRegistry& Lib
"advapi32.dll" Alias "RegConnectRegistryA"
(ByVal lpMachineName$, ByVal hkey&, phkResult&)
```

In this definition, the character & is a type definition character. A type definition character appended to a variable name indicates the variable's data type. For example, RegConnectRegistry& indicates that RegConnectRegistry will return the long data type. Some of the other data types are listed in Table 4.1.

Table 4.1 Type Definition Characters

Character	Data Type
%	Integer
$	String
!	Single
#	Double
@	Currency

Note: Not every data type has a type-definition character; for example, the data types Boolean, Byte, Data, Object, and Variant do not.

In 32-bit Visual Basic, functions exposed by the DLLs are case sensitive, while in 16-bit Visual Basic, they aren't. The Alias clause can be used to override case sensitivity in function names as long as the alias name refers to the same name of the procedure in the DLL. Here's a hypothetical declaration statement for person A:

```
Declare Function RegSetValueEx& Lib "advapi32.dll"
Alias "RegSetValueExA" (ByVal hkey&, ByVal
lpszValueName$, ByVal dwRes&, ByVal dwType&,
lpDataBuff As Byte, ByVal nSize&)
```

and for person B:

```
Declare Function REGSETVALUEEX& Lib "advapi32.dll"
Alias "RegSetValueExA" (ByVal hkey&, ByVal
lpszValueName$, ByVal dwRes&, ByVal dwType&,
lpDataBuff As Byte, ByVal nSize&)
```

In these example declarations, RegSetValueEx and REGSETVALUEEX refer to the same function: RegSetValueExA within advapi32.dll.

RegSetValueExA represents the ANSI version of RegSetValueEx, as can be seen in the following extract from winreg.h in Visual C++ 4.*x*:

```
#ifdef UNICODE
#define RegSetValueEx   RegSetValueExW
#else
#define RegSetValueEx   RegSetValueExA
#endif // !UNICODE
```

The Unicode version of the RegSetValueEx is RegSetValueExW.

The ANSI version of the RegSetValueEx function is used in the Visual Basic declaration because Visual Basic converts the internal Unicode string to ANSI for all API/DLL calls made via declare statements. In other words, Visual Basic maintains a variable-length string internally as Unicode, except when a **type library** is used. A type library is a file that contains standard descriptions of methods, properties, and events exposed by the OLE objects.

16-bit Visual Basic uses the *Pascal calling convention*, while 32-bit Visual Basic uses the *Stdcall calling convention*. Both versions pass the actual value on the stack when an argument is passed as ByVal. If an argument is passed as ByRef, a pointer to the value is passed. Note that this rule applies only to arguments that are not of the string type.

When a string is passed as ByVal, for example, as "ByVal lpszValueName$," Visual Basic passes a pointer to the beginning of the string data specified at the address lpszValueName. When a string is passed as ByRef, Visual Basic passes an indirect pointer to the string.

For more information on these calling conventions, refer to the file vb4dll.txt provided with Visual Basic 4.0.

The Registry API function declarations, types, and constants can be found in the file reg.bas under chapter 4\vbreg on the accompanying disk.

Creating a Key and Setting Its Value

In this section, we give an example of how to create a key and its values using both C and Visual Basic. The example creates a subkey called TEST under HKEY_LOCAL_MACHINE\SOFTWARE. TEST has four values, each of which has its own data type. Figure 4.2 shows TEST and its values.

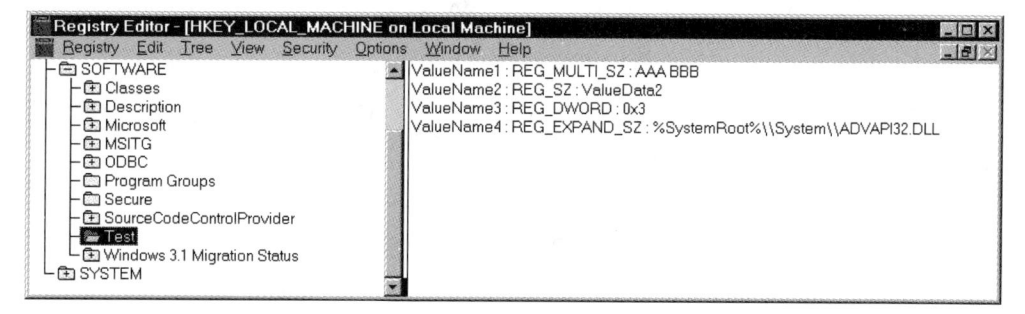

Figure 4.2 Key TEST and its values

In Figure 4.2, the first value, ValueName1, has data type REG_MULTI_SZ. Its value data contains two strings: "AAA" and "BBB." The second value, ValueName2, has data type REG_SZ. Its value data is the string "ValueData2."

The third value, ValueName3, has the data type REG_DWORD. Its value data is decimal 3. The fourth value, ValueName4, has data type REG_EXPAND_SZ. Its value data is the string "%SystemRoot%\\ System\\ADVAPI32.DLL."

Let's take a look at how to programmatically create the key TEST and set its values using both C and Visual Basic. Listing 4.7 highlights the code for using RegCreateKeyEx and RegSetValueEx to create a key and set its values using C.

Note: All the code listed in this chapter is abridged to emphasize the essential parts. You can find the complete project in the chapter 4\vcreg directory on the accompanying disk.

Listing 4.7
```
HKEY hTestKey;
ULONG lpDisposition;
BYTE bValueData[MAX_PATH];
char szValueData[MAX_PATH];
CString msg;

if(ERROR_SUCCESS != RegCreateKeyEx(HKEY_LOCAL_MACHINE,
                "SOFTWARE\\TEST",
                0,
                NULL,
                REG_OPTION_NON_VOLATILE,
                KEY_ALL_ACCESS,
```

```
                        NULL,
                        &hTestKey,
                        &lpDisposition))

{
   msg.Format("Could not create key Test.  Error code
            %ld.\n", GetLastError());
   AfxMessageBox(msg);
   return;
}


//'A''A''A''\0''B''B''B''\0''\0'
memset(bValueData, 'A', 3);
memset(bValueData+3,'\0',1);
memset(bValueData+4, 'B',3);
memset(bValueData+7, '\0',2);



if(ERROR_SUCCESS !=
            RegSetValueEx(hTestKey,   // subkey handle
            "ValueName1",             // value name
            0,                        // must be zero
            REG_MULTI_SZ,             // value type
            (LPBYTE)bValueData,       // address of value data
            9))                       // length of value data
{
   msg.Format("Could not set value(ValueName1).
            Error code %ld.\n", GetLastError());
   AfxMessageBox(msg);
   return;
}



if(ERROR_SUCCESS != RegSetValueEx(hTestKey,
                    "ValueName2", 0, REG_SZ,
                    (const BYTE* )"ValueData2",
                    strlen("ValueData2")+1))
{
```

```
    msg.Format("Could not set value(ValueName2).
            Error code %ld.\n", GetLastError());
    AfxMessageBox(msg);
    return;
}


int nValue = 3;
if(ERROR_SUCCESS != RegSetValueEx(hTestKey,
                    "ValueName3", 0, REG_DWORD,
                    (const BYTE*) &nValue,
                    sizeof(nValue)))
{
    msg.Format("Could not set value(ValueName3) .
            Error code %ld.\n", GetLastError());
    AfxMessageBox(msg);
    return;
}


strcpy(szValueData, "%SystemRoot%\\System
        \\TCASVC.dll");

if(ERROR_SUCCESS != RegSetValueEx(hTestKey,
                    "ValueName4",
                    0,
                    REG_EXPAND_SZ,
                    (LPBYTE)szValueData,
                    strlen(szValueData) + 1))
{
msg.Format("Could not set value(ValueName4) .
            Error code %ld.\n",GetLastError());
AfxMessageBox(msg);
return;
}

RegCloseKey(hTestKey);

AfxMessageBox("Successfully done");
```

When a value is set with value type REG_DWORD, as in the previous listing, nValue must be casted to a byte pointer, as follows:

```
int nValue = 3;
    if(ERROR_SUCCESS != RegSetValueEx(hTestKey,
            "ValueName3", 0, REG_DWORD,
            (const BYTE*)&nValue, sizeof(nValue)))
```

For the value type REG_MULTI_SZ, each string in the byte array must be terminated with a NULL terminating character. The last string in the byte array must end with two NULL terminating characters.

Listing 4.8 highlights the corresponding implementation using Visual Basic.

Listing 4.8

```
Dim lret As Long
Dim hKeyServer As Long
Dim hKeyTest As Long
Dim nullstr As String
Dim szSourceKey As String
Dim szValueName As String
Dim bValueData(512) As Byte ' 512 character limit
Dim lRetValue As Long
Dim lpSecurity As SECURITY_ATTRIBUTES

lret = RegConnectRegistry(Chr(0), HKEY_LOCAL_MACHINE, _
        hKeyServer) 'CHR(0)
If (lret <> ERROR_SUCCESS) Then
    MsgBox "RegConnectRegistry Failed"
    Exit Sub
End If

szSourceKey = "SOFTWARE\TEST"

lret = RegCreateKeyEx(hKeyServer, szSourceKey, 0,_
        Chr(0), REG_OPTION_NON_VOLATILE, _
        KEY_ALL_ACCESS, lpSecurity, hKeyTest, lRetValue)
```

```
If (lret <> ERROR_SUCCESS) Then
    MsgBox "RegCreateKeyEx Failed"
    Exit Sub
End If

Dim lByteLen As Long

szValueData = "AAA"
For i = 0 To Len(szValueData) - 1
    bValueData(i) = Asc(Mid(szValueData, i + 1, 1))
Next i
bValueData(i + 1) = Asc(Chr(0))

szValueData = "BBB"
For j = i + 1 To i + 1 + Len(szValueData) - 1
    bValueData(j) = Asc(Mid(szValueData, j - i, 1))
Next j
bValueData(j + 1) = Asc(Chr(0))
bValueData(j + 2) = Asc(Chr(0))

lret = RegSetValueEx(hKeyTest, "ValueName1", 0, _
        REG_MULTI_SZ, bValueData(0), j + 2)
If (lret <> ERROR_SUCCESS) Then
    MsgBox "RegSetValueEx failed"
    Exit Sub
End If

szValueData = "ValueData2"

For j = 0 To Len(szValueData) - 1
    bValueData(j) = Asc(Mid(szValueData, j + 1, 1))
Next j
bValueData(j + 1) = Asc(Chr(0))

lret = RegSetValueEx(hKeyTest, "ValueName2", 0, _
        REG_SZ, bValueData(0), j + 1)
```

```
Dim lData As Long

lData = 3
lret = RegSetValueDWord(hKeyTest, "ValueName3", 0, _
        REG_DWORD, lData, 4)
If (lret <> ERROR_SUCCESS) Then
    MsgBox "RegSetValueDWord failed"
    Exit Sub
End If

szValueData = "%SystemRoot%\System\ADVAPI.DLL"
For j = 0 To Len(szValueData) - 1
    bValueData(j) = Asc(Mid(szValueData, j + 1, 1))
Next j
bValueData(j + 1) = Asc(Chr(0))

lret = RegSetValueEx(hKeyTest, "ValueName4", 0, _
        REG_EXPAND_SZ, bValueData(0), j + 1)

MsgBox "Successfully done"
```

Note: This Visual Basic code can be found in the chapter 4\vbreg directory on the accompanying disk.

RegConnectRegistry will establish a connection on a predefined handle on another machine. This API has three parameters:

```
RegConnectRegistry(
  LPTSTR lpMachineName,   // address of remote computer
                          // name
  HKEY hKey,              // predefined registry handle
  PHKEY phResult)         // remote registry handle
```

The predefined handles that can be accessed on the remote machine are HKEY_LOCAL_MACHINE and HKEY_USERS. If the address of the lpMachineName is chr(0) (which is equivalent to a NULL character in C), a handle will be returned to the local machine.

There is no pointer concept in Visual Basic as there is in C. Because the Registry APIs are declared in the C language, when a parameter is declared in the API as a pointer you can pass either the first element of the Byte array or pass a string as ByVal.

The following code shows an example of passing a string through Visual Basic:

```
lret = RegSetValueEx(hKeyTest, szValueName, 0, _
        REG_MULTI_SZ, szValueData(0), j + 2)
```

In particular, szValueName is the buffer that contains the value name. szValueName is defined as a string as follows:

```
Dim szValueName as String
```

The buffer space can be allocated by adding the statement

```
szValueName = space$(40)
```

Here, 40 is the number of spaces (characters) in the string. szValueData is the buffer that contains the value data. It is defined as

```
Dim ValueData(512) As Byte ' 512 character limit
```

ValueData is defined as type Byte so that it is consistent with the RegSetValueEx function declaration:

```
Declare Function RegSetValueEx& Lib "advapi32.dll" _
Alias "RegSetValueExA" (ByVal hkey&, ByVal _
lpszValueName$, ByVal dwRes&, ByVal dwType&, _
lpDataBuff As Byte, ByVal nSize&)
```

In this declaration, lpDataBuff is defined as type Byte. The Byte array type must be used when the value type is REG_MULTI_SZ, since a REG_MULTI_SZ is an array of NULL-terminated strings that is terminated by an additional NULL terminator. The Byte array also is used to prevent the type checking, so you can pass either a string or a NULL pointer.

RegSetValueEx's declaration above also can be used for the value type REG_SZ, since REG_SZ is a NULL-terminated string. It further can be used for value type REG_EXPAND_SZ, since its value data also is a NULL-terminated string that contains unexpanded references to environment variables such as %PATH%.

For value type REG_DWORD, it is much easier to declare the RegSetValueEx function prototype as follows:

```
Declare Function RegSetValueDWord& Lib "advapi32" _
Alias "RegSetValueExA" (ByVal hkey&, ByVal _
lpValueName$, ByVal Reserved&, ByVal dwType&, _
lpData&, ByVal cbData&)
```

However, notice that the RegSetValueEx declaration and the RegSetValueDWord declaration differ in that the value data parameter is defined as lpData& in RegSetValueDWord, whereas lpDataBuffer is defined as Byte in RegSetValueEx. If the value type is REG_DWORD, using RegSetValueDWord will make manipulating the data much easier.

For RegSetValueEx, it is very important to pass the exact length of the value data (ByVal nSize&) in RegSetValueEx so that the correct value can be written to the Registry.

Besides setting the value, you also can query the data associated with the named value. The following section demonstrates how to properly use RegQueryValueEx to retrieve the value data using both the C and Visual Basic languages.

Querying a Value

Listing 4.9 shows the use of RegQueryValueEx within C. The listing below queries the value of ValueName2.

Listing 4.9
```
HKEY hTestKey;
DWORD dwValueType;
DWORD dwValueLen;
BYTE bValueData[MAX_PATH];
int nRet;
CString msg;
```

```
if(ERROR_SUCCESS != RegOpenKeyEx(HKEY_LOCAL_MACHINE,
                                 "SOFTWARE\\TEST",
                                 0,
                                 KEY_ALL_ACCESS,
                                 &hTestKey))
{
   msg.Format("Could not open key(HKEY_LOCAL_MACHINE
              \\SOFTWARE\\TEST). Error code %ld.\n",
              GetLastError());
   AfxMessageBox(msg);
   return;
}

dwValueLen = sizeof(bValueData);

nRet = RegQueryValueEx(hTestKey,
                       "ValueName2",
                       0,
                       &dwValueType ,
                       (LPBYTE)bValueData,
                       &dwValueLen);

if(nRet != ERROR_SUCCESS)
{
   msg.Format("Could not QueryValue(ValueName2).
              Error code %ld.\n",GetLastError());
   AfxMessageBox(msg);
   return;
}

switch(dwValueType)
{
   case REG_SZ:
      msg.Format("ValueName2: REG_SZ: %s\n",
                 bValueData);
      AfxMessageBox(msg);
      break;
```

```
   case REG_DWORD:
      msg.Format("ValueName2: REG_DWORD: %d\n",
                  *(UINT *)bValueData);
      AfxMessageBox(msg);
      break;
   default:
      break;
}


RegCloseKey(hTestKey);
```

It is very important to allocate a buffer for the returned value data; otherwise, the value data may not be retrieved properly.

Listing 4.10 shows the usage of RegQueryValueEx in Visual Basic.

Listing 4.10

```
Dim lret As Long
Dim hTestKey As Long
Dim dwValueLen As Long
Dim szValueData As String

szValueData = Space(100)
dwValueLen = Len(szValueData)
lret = RegOpenKeyEx(HKEY_LOCAL_MACHINE, _
        "SOFTWARE\TEST", 0, KEY_ALL_ACCESS, hTestKey)
If (lret <> ERROR_SUCCESS) Then
   MsgBox "RegOpenKeyEx failed"
   Exit Sub
End If


'dwValueLen counts the null terminator
lret = RegQueryValueEx(hTestKey, "ValueName2", 0, _
        REG_SZ, szValueData, dwValueLen)
If (lret <> ERROR_SUCCESS) Then
   MsgBox "RegQueryValueEx failed"
   Exit Sub
End If
```

```
szValueData = Left(szValueData, dwValueLen - 1)
MsgBox "ValueName2: REG_SZ: " & szValueData
RegCloseKey (hkey)
```

It is very important to allocate a buffer for the returned value data; otherwise, a General Protection Fault might occur. When you are manipulating different value types, proper function declarations will dictate how you can manipulate them. For example, RegQueryValueEx's declaration in Visual Basic:

```
Declare Function RegQueryValueEx& Lib _
"advapi32.dll" Alias "RegQueryValueExA" _
(ByVal hkey&, ByVal lpszValueName$, ByVal lpdwRes&, _
lpdwType&, ByVal lpDataBuff$, nSize&)
```

is best used for the value type REG_MUTLI_SZ. Yet, for the data type REG_SZ, the declaration

```
ByVal  lpDataBuff  as String
```

would be better. And for the data type REG_DWORD, lpDataBuff can be declared as

```
ByVal lpDataBuff  as long
```

Note: It is very important that whenever a key is not used, the key handle is closed by calling RegCloseKey, since the key handle is part of the system resource.

To enumerate all the values associated with a specified key, you can use RegEnumValue, which is the topic of the next section.

Enumerating Values

Listing 4.11 shows the usage of the function RegEnumValue in C. It enumerates all of the values associated within the key SOFTWARE\TEST.

Listing 4.11

```
HKEY hTestKey;
DWORD dwValueType;
DWORD dwValueNameLen;
DWORD dwValueDataLen;
BYTE bValueData[MAX_PATH];
char szValueName[MAX_PATH];
int nRet;
int nIndex;
char *ptr;
CString msg;
CString strWholeMsg;
CString strTemp;


if(ERROR_SUCCESS != RegOpenKeyEx(HKEY_LOCAL_MACHINE,
                                 "SOFTWARE\\TEST",
                                 0,
                                 KEY_ALL_ACCESS,
                                 &hTestKey))
{
   msg.Format("Could not open key(HKEY_LOCAL_MACHINE
            \\SOFTWARE\\TEST). Error code %ld.\n",
            GetLastError());
   AfxMessageBox(msg);
   return;
}

nIndex = 0;

while(1)
{
   dwValueNameLen = sizeof(szValueName);
   dwValueDataLen = sizeof(bValueData);


   nRet = RegEnumValue(hTestKey,
                       nIndex,
                       szValueName,
```

```
                     &dwValueNameLen,
                     0,
                     &dwValueType,
                     (LPBYTE)bValueData,
                     &dwValueDataLen);
if(nRet == ERROR_NO_MORE_ITEMS)
   break;
else if(nRet != ERROR_SUCCESS)
{
   msg.Format("Could not enum value. Error code
            %ld.\n",GetLastError());
   AfxMessageBox(msg);
   return;
}

switch(dwValueType)
{
   case REG_DWORD:
      msg.Format("%s: REG_DWORD : %d\n", szValueName,
               *(UINT *)bValueData);
      break;
   case REG_SZ:
      msg.Format("%s: REG_SZ : %s\n", szValueName,
               bValueData);
      break;
   case REG_EXPAND_SZ:
      msg.Format("%s: REG_EXPAND_SZ : %s\n",
               szValueName, bValueData);
      break;
   case REG_MULTI_SZ:
      ptr = (char*)bValueData;msg.Format("%s:
            REG_MULTI_SZ: ", szValueName);
      while (*ptr)
      {
         strTemp.Format("%s: ", ptr);
         ptr += strlen(ptr)+1;
         msg += strTemp;
      }
```

```
            msg = msg + "\n";
            break;
        default:
            break;
    }
    nIndex++;
    strWholeMsg += msg;
}


AfxMessageBox(strWholeMsg);


RegCloseKey(hTestKey);
```

Note: It is critical that the value name length and the value data length be initialized each time before RegEnumValue is invoked; otherwise, the value name and value data will not return proper data.

Notice the following lines from Listing 4.11:

```
case REG_DWORD:
    msg.Format("%s: REG_DWORD : %d\n", szValueName,
                *(UINT *)bValueData);
        break;
```

It is very important that byte array bValueData be cast as a UINT for data type REG_DWORD so that the proper value can be retrieved.

Listing 4.12 shows the usage of RegEnumValue within Visual Basic.

Listing 4.12
```
Dim lret As Long
Dim hTestKey As Long
Dim nIndex As Long
Dim dwValueDataLen As Long
Dim dwValueNameLen As Long
Dim szValueName As String
Dim bValueData(512) As Byte ' 512 character limit
Dim dwValueType As Long

szValueName = Space$(100)
```

```
lret = RegOpenKeyEx(HKEY_LOCAL_MACHINE, _
        "SOFTWARE\TEST", 0, KEY_READ, hTestKey)
If lret <> ERROR_SUCCESS Then
    MsgBox "RegOpenKeyEx failed"
    Exit Sub
End If

nIndex = 0

Do
    dwValueNameLen = Len(szValueName)
    dwValueDataLen = 512
    lret = RegEnumValue(hTestKey, nIndex, _
            szValueName, dwValueNameLen, _
            0, dwValueType&, bValueData(0), _
            dwValueDataLen)
    If (lret <> ERROR_NO_MORE_ITEMS) Then
        GoTo EnumStop:
    End If

    If (lret <> ERROR_SUCCESS) Then
        MsgBox "RegEnumValue failed"
        Exit Sub
    End If

    nIndex = nIndex + 1
Loop Until (lret <> ERROR_NO_MORE_ITEMS)
EnumStop:
    MsgBox "Successfully done"
```

Note: In the C language example, the path SOFTWARE\\TEST was used, while in the Visual Basic version, the path SOFTWARE\TEST was used. This is because the \ character requires a second \ when it is embedded in a C language string type.

To enumerate all the subkeys that belong to a particular key, you use RegEnumKeyEx. This function is very useful when you want to delete a key that has subkeys. In the Windows 95 environment, a key, along with its subkeys, can be deleted using the function RegDeleteKey. However, in

Windows NT RegDeleteKey will not delete a key that has subkeys. However, it will delete all *values* associated with the key.

The following section demonstrates how to delete a key that has subkeys.

Deleting a Key That Has Subkeys

Listing 4.13 shows how to delete a key that has subkeys by using the C language. The following operations are performed:

1. Create a TEST subkey called SUBTEST.

2. Create some name-value pairs for SUBTEST.

3. Call RegEnumKey to enumerate TEST's subkey.

4. Delete TEST's subkey.

Listing 4.13
```
HKEY hTestKey;
HKEY hSubTestKey;
int nRet;
int nIndex;
char szKeyName[256];
CString msg;


if(ERROR_SUCCESS != RegOpenKeyEx(HKEY_LOCAL_MACHINE,
                                 "SOFTWARE\\TEST",
                                 0,
                                 KEY_ALL_ACCESS,
                                 &hTestKey))
{
   msg.Format("Could not open key(HKEY_LOCAL_MACHINE
           \\SOFTWARE\\TEST). Error code %ld.\n",
           GetLastError());
   AfxMessageBox(msg);
   return;
}
```

```
if(ERROR_SUCCESS != RegCreateKeyEx(hTestKey,
                    "SUBTEST",
                    0,
                    NULL,
                    REG_OPTION_NON_VOLATILE,
                    KEY_ALL_ACCESS,
                    NULL,
                    &hSubTestKey,
                    NULL))
{
   msg.Format("Could not create key(HKEY_LOCAL_MACHINE
            \\SOFTWARE\\TEST\\SUBTEST). Error code
            %ld.\n", GetLastError());
   AfxMessageBox(msg);
   return;
}


if(ERROR_SUCCESS != RegSetValueEx(hSubTestKey,
                    "SubValueName1", 0, REG_SZ,
                    (LPBYTE)"SubValueData1",
                    strlen("SubValueData1")+1))

{
   msg.Format("Could not set value(SubValueName1).
            Error code %ld.\n",GetLastError());
   AfxMessageBox(msg);
   return;
}

nIndex=0;

//delete all the subkeys contained by key TEST.
while(1)
{
   nRet =    RegEnumKey(hTestKey,
                    nIndex,
                    szKeyName,
                    sizeof(szKeyName));
```

```
    if(nRet == ERROR_NO_MORE_ITEMS)
        break;
    else if(nRet != ERROR_SUCCESS)
    {
        msg.Format("Could not enum key(SUBTESTKEY).
                    Error code %ld.\n",GetLastError());
        AfxMessageBox(msg);
        return;
    }

    if(ERROR_SUCCESS != RegDeleteKey(hTestKey, szKeyName))
    {
        msg.Format("Could not delete key(SUBTESTKEY).
                    Error code %ld.\n",GetLastError());
        AfxMessageBox(msg);
        return;
    }
    nIndex++;

}


//delete key will automatically delete all the values
//associated with the key.
//but not the subkeys it contains.
RegDeleteKey(HKEY_LOCAL_MACHINE, "SOFTWARE\\TEST");
AfxMessageBox("Successfully done");
```

Listing 4.14 shows how to delete a key that has subkeys by using Visual Basic.

Listing 4.14
```
Dim hTestKey As Long
Dim hSubTestKey As Long
Dim lret As Long
Dim szValueData As String
Dim nIndex As Long
Dim szKeyName As String
Dim lpSecurity As SECURITY_ATTRIBUTES
```

```
Dim lRetValue As Long
Dim bValueData(512) As Byte


lret = RegOpenKeyEx(HKEY_LOCAL_MACHINE, _
        "SOFTWARE\TEST", 0, KEY_ALL_ACCESS, hTestKey)
If (lret <> ERROR_SUCCESS) Then
   MsgBox "RegOpenKeyEx failed"
   Exit Sub
End If

lret = RegCreateKeyEx(hTestKey, "SUBTEST", 0, Chr(0), _
        REG_OPTION_NON_VOLATILE, KEY_ALL_ACCESS, _
        lpSecurity, hSubTestKey, lRetValue)
If (lret <> ERROR_SUCCESS) Then
   MsgBox "RegCreateKeyEx failed"
   Exit Sub
End If


szValueData = "SubValueData1"
For j = 0 To Len(szValueData) - 1
   bValueData(j) = Asc(Mid(szValueData, j + 1, 1))
Next j
bValueData(j + 1) = Asc(Chr(0))

lret = RegSetValueEx(hSubTestKey, "SubValueName1", 0, _
        REG_SZ,  bValueData(0), j + 1)
If (lret <> ERROR_SUCCESS) Then
   MsgBox "RegSetValueEx failed"
   Exit Sub
End If

Dim dwKeyLen As Long

szKeyName = Space$(100)
dwKeyLen = Len(szKeyName)
```

```
Do
    lret = RegEnumKey(hTestKey, nIndex, szKeyName, _
        dwKeyLen)

    lret = RegDeleteKey(hTestKey, Left(szKeyName, _
        dwKeyLen - 1))

    nIndex = nIndex + 1
Loop Until (lret <> ERROR_NO_MORE_ITEMS)

lret = RegDeleteKey(HKEY_LOCAL_MACHINE, "SOFTWARE\TEST")
If (lret <> ERROR_SUCCESS) Then
    MsgBox "RegDeleteKey failed"
    Exit Sub
End If
MsgBox "Successfully done"
```

To properly use RegEnumKey, you must allocate buffer space for the returned key name before invoking RegEnumKey. In Listing 4.14, the following code is used to allocate this buffer:

```
szKeyName = Space$(100)
```

Note: dwKeyLen returned from RegEnumKey is the length of the key name, including the NULL terminator. To properly retrieve the key name, the following code can be invoked:

```
Left(szKeyName, dwKeyLen -1 )
```

Summary

There are a few caveats when using theWin32 Registry API in Visual Basic and C applications:

■ Proper declare statements when using the Registry APIs from Visual Basic are a must.

- Registry keys and their handles are system resources. They should be freed appropriately when they are no longer used in your application.

- Both 16-bit and 32-bit versions of most functions are available.

- Both ANSI and UNICODE versions of most functions are available.

- You must declare constants, types, and function prototypes of the Registry API before using them.

- Buffer space allocation and proper data types are the keys to successful manipulation of Registry APIs in Visual Basic.

- REG_MUTI_SZ value types require a special format, as cited in the chapter.

Chapter 5

C++ Examples of the Registry API

Any application can use the Registry to store configuration or state information. Certain applications use the Registry as a way of communicating with other applications. For example, the Event Log knows which applications can be monitored because those applications create a Registry entry within the Event Log's Registry key.

In this chapter, we discuss how to implement the DllRegisterServer and DllUnregisterServer API and give examples of using the Performance Monitor and the Event Log. DllRegisterServer and DllUnregisterServer API are the standard methods for implementing a DLL that registers.

Registering and Unregistering DLLs

Many DLLs depend on the Registry for configuration information. Some use entries that already exist on the machine, either placed there by other applications or by the operating system. Most insert keys and name-value pairs into the Registry that only they will use. Some DLLs will not run without the appropriate keys in place.

It would seem then that the DLL would create these keys every time the DLL was loaded. This is not the case, however, because modifying the Registry every time a DLL is loaded is costly. So a DLL modifies the Registry only once. The one-time modification is called **registering.** Registering is done by exporting an API called DllRegisterServer. This API is usually called by the setup program when the DLL is installed so that the correct keys are created.

Registering a DLL

A utility called regsvr32.exe that ships with Windows NT and Windows 95 calls the exported DllRegisterServer API. It is usually run from the command line. Typically users do not have to register DLLs themselves using regsvr32.exe. However, they may need to sometime. In which case, the user would enter the following on the command line:

```
regsvr32 mydll.dll
```

A pop-up box then would appear indicating whether the DLL successfully registered. The DLL might not register successfully for various reasons, including poor programming and missing components. Whether it does depends on the return code the DllRegisterServer API returns to regsvr32.exe. Return codes are discussed later in the chapter.

If you do not want the pop-up box to appear, such as in batch processing, you can add a switch, /s, as in this example:

```
regsvr32 /s mydll.dll
```

Unregistering a DLL

DLLs also can be unregistered. Doing this involves having the DLL remove the Registry entries it created when registering. Unregistering can be useful when trying to remove an installed DLL so as to replace it with a later version. Unregistering a DLL requires the DLL to have exported a procedure called DllUnRegisterServer. To call DllUnRegisterServer, you use regsvr32.exe with a /u switch, like this:

```
regsvr32 /u mydll.dll
```

Implementing a DLL That Registers

To implement a DLL that registers, you must implement the DllRegisterServer API. In that API, you need to use the Registry API code given earlier in the book to configure the Registry. You also need to return S_OK if the registration process went successfully or E_UNEXPECTED if it went unsuccessfully. By using these return codes, you can signal regsvr32.exe to display the appropriate pop-up box.

Listing 5.1 shows example code using a DllRegisterServer API that you could put into a DLL.

Listing 5.1

```
STDAPI DllRegisterServer(void)
{
HKEY  hkKey=NULL;

if (RegCreateKey(
HKEY_LOCAL_MACHINE,
"SYSTEM\\CurrentControlSet\\Services\\EventLog
\\Application\\TestApp",
&hkKey)!=ERROR_SUCCESS)
{
return (E_UNEXPECTED);
}

if (RegSetValue(hkKey,NULL, REG_SZ,"Foo",_tcslen("Foo")
)!=ERROR_SUCCESS)
{
if (hkKey)
RegCloseKey(hkKey);

return (E_UNEXPECTED);
}

if (hkKey)
RegCloseKey(hkKey);

return (S_OK);
}
```

Implementing a DLL That Unregisters

To implement a DLL that unregisters, you must implement the DllUnregisterServer API and use the same error codes as used with DllRegisterServer, plus one other: S_FALSE. Returning S_FALSE means the DllUnregisterServer will remove all known Registry keys and name-value pairs, although other Registry entries might exist.

Listing 5.2 shows example code using a DllUnregisterServer API that you could put into a DLL. The example deletes the keys created in Listing 5.1.

Listing 5.2

```
STDAPI DllUnregisterServer(void)
{
if (RegDeleteKey(
HKEY_LOCAL_MACHINE,
"SYSTEM\\CurrentControlSet\\Services\\EventLog
\\Application\\TestApp"
))
{
return (E_UNEXPECTED);
}
return (S_OK);
}
```

Registering and Unregistering ActiveX Controls

ActiveX controls also can be registered and unregistered. These controls are discussed at length in Chapter 6. Contained in OCXs, they can export both the DllRegisterServer and DllUnregisterServer; regsvr32.exe works with OCXs in the same way it works with DLLs.

Listing 5.3 shows example code using DllRegisterServer in an ActiveX control.

Listing 5.3

```
STDAPI DllRegisterServer(void)
{
AFX_MANAGE_STATE(_afxModuleAddrThis);

if (!AfxOleRegisterTypeLib(AfxGetInstanceHandle(),
_tlid))
return ResultFromScode(SELFREG_E_TYPELIB);

if (!COleObjectFactoryEx::UpdateRegistryAll(TRUE))
return ResultFromScode(SELFREG_E_CLASS);
```

```
return NOERROR;
}
```

Listing 5.4 shows example code using DllUnregisterServer for the same Active X control in Listing 5.3.

Listing 5.4

```
STDAPI DllUnregisterServer(void)
{
  AFX_MANAGE_STATE(_afxModuleAddrThis);

  if (!AfxOleUnregisterTypeLib(_tlid, _wVerMajor,
  _wVerMinor))
    return ResultFromScode(SELFREG_E_TYPELIB);

  if (!COleObjectFactoryEx::UpdateRegistryAll(FALSE))
    return ResultFromScode(SELFREG_E_CLASS);

  return NOERROR;
}
```

Registering Executables

There is no way for an executable to export procedures like DLL or OCXs, so an executable must self-register via the command line /REGSERVER. To register an executable, call it as follows:

```
regexe.exe /REGSERVER
```

Calling an executable this way would be the equivalent of calling DllRegisterServer in a DLL. The executable should not perform its developed task; it should only make Registry adjustments.

Listing 5.5 shows example code for registering an executable.

Listing 5.5

```
#include <Stdio.h>
#include <string.h>
```

```cpp
#include <afx.h>
#include <winreg.h>

int main( int argc, char *argv[ ], char *envp[ ] )
{
// Section for Registering

if (argc==2)
{
if (!strcmp(argv[1],"/REGSERVER"))
{
HKEY  hkKey=NULL;

if (RegCreateKey(
HKEY_LOCAL_MACHINE,
"SOFTWARE\\Widget Ware\\TestApp",
&hkKey)!=ERROR_SUCCESS)
{
return (1);
}

if (RegSetValue(hkKey,NULL, REG_SZ,"Foo",_tcslen("Foo")
)!=ERROR_SUCCESS)
{
if (hkKey)
RegCloseKey(hkKey);

return (1);
}

if (hkKey)
RegCloseKey(hkKey);

return(0);
}
}

// Normal Code
```

```
return(0);
}
```

Unregistering Executables

Unregistering an executable is a lot like registering one. Instead of calling the executable with the switch /REGSERVER, you call it with the switch /UNREGSERVER. Here is an example:

```
regexe.exe /UNREGSERVER
```

Listing 5.6 shows example code for unregistering an executable by just adding onto the code in Listing 5.5.

Listing 5.6

```
#include <Stdio.h>
#include <string.h>
#include <afx.h>
#include <winreg.h>

int main( int argc, char *argv[ ], char *envp[ ] )
{
// Section for Registering

if (argc==2)
{
// Registering the Execuatable

if (!strcmp(argv[1],"/REGSERVER"))
{
HKEY   hkKey=NULL;

if (RegCreateKey(
HKEY_LOCAL_MACHINE,
"SOFTWARE\\Widget Ware\\TestApp",
&hkKey)!=ERROR_SUCCESS)
{
return (1);
}
```

```
if (RegSetValue(hkKey,NULL, REG_SZ,"Foo",_tcslen("Foo")
)!=ERROR_SUCCESS)
{
if (hkKey)
RegCloseKey(hkKey);

return (1);
}

if (hkKey)
RegCloseKey(hkKey);

return(0);
}

// Unregistering the Execuatable

if (!strcmp(argv[1],"/UNREGSERVER"))
{
if (RegDeleteKey(
HKEY_LOCAL_MACHINE,
"SOFTWARE\\Widget Ware\\TestApp")!=ERROR_SUCCESS)
{
return (1);
}

return(0);
}

}

// Normal Code

return(0);
}
```

The Event Log

The Event Log is a way for services and other applications that do not have a GUI to write out information to the user. Usually, the Log is used to write error messages from a service to the system's administrator. It consists of messages that actually are written to three different logs: the System Log, the Security Log, and the Application Log.

The System Log consists of messages about system processes and services, the Security Log consists of messages about security issues, and the Application Log consists of messages about applications. Each log breaks down its messages according to the source of the message and each source by category. Each message logged to the Event Log can be one of three severity levels: error, warning, and informational.

NT Server comes with an application to view the Event Log. It is called the Event Viewer and can be found in the Administrators Tools. The Event Viewer is organized as a table, which is reproduced in Table 5.1. Double-click a row to see the message logged for that row.

Table 5.1 Event Viewer categories

Row	Message
Severity	A blue, yellow, or red dot indicating the severity level of the error. Blue is informational, yellow is warning, and red is error.
Date	The date the message was written to the Event Log.
Time	The time the message was written to the Event Log.
Source	The name of the application or service that generated the error.
Category	The source's category for the error.
Event	The ID of the message.
Users	The user under whom the application is running. If the application is running under the system, this will appear as unknown.
Computer	The computer that filed the error.

How the Registry Comes into Play in the Event Log

For an application to use Windows' APIs to write messages to the Event Log, it first must be registered with the Event Log. You do this by making some Registry entries. Before registering anything with the Log, however, you should understand how the messages get written.

When an application uses a Windows API to write to the Event Log, it passes an ID to a string rather than a string to the API. Each ID and string are defined in a message file that is part of the application's resource. This means that each message that the application writes to the Event Log is predefined in that application's resource. When Windows receives the ID to the message, it writes the ID, not the message, to the Event Log. This allows the Event Log to remain very small.

When the Event Viewer is opened, it reads the Registry and figures out which DLLs have message files for which sources. When you double-click a row in the Event Log, the Log loads the DLL and reads the message section of the resource that pertains to the message ID.

Categories work in much the same way. When the application uses the Windows API to write to the Event Log, an ID is used. This ID refers to a message contained in the message section in the application's resource. When the Event Viewer is loaded, it references the Registry for all the DLLs of every source that has a row in the table. The Event Viewer then loads the DLLs and reads the name of the category from the DLL using the ID as a reference.

Usually, the same application is used for both the categories and the messages. Each application may have only one message section in its resource, so the messages and categories end up in the same message section. To distinguish between messages and categories, an entry is placed in the Registry that indicates the numbers of the categories in the message section. Categories are numbered beginning with the ID of 0 and increment in units of 1. A message, on the other hand, may have any ID as long as the ID doesn't conflict with the category IDs. Usually messages start with ID 100 and go up. A good trick is to have all messages that go with Category 1 to be in the 100s, all messages that go with Category 2 to be in the 200s, and so on.

An Example Application

Let's create an application that writes to the Registry. We'll use the Project Wizard to create a simple DLL that we can use for an example. Here are the steps to follow:

1. Open Microsoft Developer Studio.

2. Click File | New.

3. Click Project Workspace.

4. Name the project EvntLog.

5. From the Type list, select MFC AppWizard (dll).

6. Select the default setting.

7. Click Create.

Creating a Message File

First, we want to create a message file that contains the messages that the application will write to the Registry. Message files are created with a special but simple syntax that is specific to the message file. The syntax must be correct, or the message compiler will not be able to compile the message.

Listing 5.7 shows example syntax of the message file.

Listing 5.7
```
MessageID=1
Facility=Application
Severity=Success
SymbolicName=EVCAT_TESTING
Language=English
Testing

.

MessageID=100
Facility=Application
Severity=Success
SymbolicName=EVMSG_MEMORY1
Language=English
Testing writing to the Registry

.
```

```
MessageID=101
Facility=Application
Severity=Error
SymbolicName=EVMSG_MEMORY2
Language=English
Testing writing to the Registry with Info: %1.
```

Each category and each message must have an entry like the previous one and each must have a different ID. Each message entry must be separated by a dot (.) and begin on a separate line. Notice that the MessageID is assigned and a SymbolicName is given. When the message file is compiled, a header file is produced. You can include the header file in your source code and reference the ID by its SymbolicName. For instance, the header file for the previous example would look like that shown in Listing 5.8.

Listing 5.8

```
//
//  Values are 32-bit values laid out as follows:
//
//   3 3 2 2 2 2 2 2 2 2 2 2 1 1 1 1 1 1 1 1 1 1
//   1 0 9 8 7 6 5 4 3 2 1 0 9 8 7 6 5 4 3 2 1 0 9 8 7 6 5 4 3 2 1 0
//  +--+-+-+---------------------+-----------------------------+
//  |Sev|C|R|       Facility      |            Code             |
//  +--+-+-+---------------------+-----------------------------+
//
//  where
//
//      Sev - is the severity code
//
//          00 - Success
//          01 - Informational
//          10 - Warning
//          11 - Error
//
//      C - is the Customer code flag
//
//      R - is a reserved bit
//
//      Facility - is the facility code
```

```
//
//          Code - is the facility's status code
//
//
// Define the facility codes
//


//
// Define the severity codes
//


//
// MessageID: EVCAT_TESTING
//
// MessageText:
//
//  Testing
//
#define EVCAT_TESTING                   0x00000001L

//
// MessageID: EVMSG_MEMORY1
//
// MessageText:
//
//  Testing writing to the Registry
//
#define EVMSG_MEMORY1                   0x00000064L

//
// MessageID: EVMSG_MEMORY2
//
// MessageText:
//
//  Testing writing to the Registry with Info: %1.
//
#define EVMSG_MEMORY2                   0xC0000065L
```

Compiling the Message File

Once you have a message file in the correct syntax, you need to compile it. This is most easily done by adding a Message Compiler tool to the Tool menu drop-down. To add this tool, follow these steps:

1. Open up Microsoft Developer Studio.

2. Click Tool | Customize.

3. Click the Tool tab.

4. Click Add. A new dialog box appears called Add Tool.

5. For the command, type c:\msdev\bin\mc.exe. This is the default location of the message compiler called mc.exe. If you have installed Microsoft Developer Studio somewhere else, you will need to use the browse option to find mc.exe.

6. Change the menu text from mc to Message Compiler.

7. Click the right arrow next to Arguments. A drop-down menu appears.

8. Click File Name from the drop-down menu.

9. Click the right arrow next to Initial Directory and select File Directory.

10. Click the check box next to "Redirect to Output Window."

11. Click Close.

Now you are done configuring the Tools menu to contain a Message Compiler tool for compiling message files. Click Tools on the Menu Bar, and you will notice that the Message Compiler tool has been added to the drop-down menu.

To compile the message file, follow these steps:

1. Open the file, ensuring it is in the front-most source window.

2. Click Tools on the Menu Bar and then click Message Compiler. The message file should compile, with the output going to the output window of Microsoft Developer Studio.

3. Save the Listing 5.7 Message File as EvntLog.mc and compile it. The compiler produces the header file plus a file called MSG00001.bin, which is used by the resource compiler. In addition, it produces an .rc file, also used by the resource compiler.

Adding the Message File to the Project

Once the message file is compiled, we add it to the project so that it can be compiled with the resources of the application. Follow these steps:

1. Click Insert | Files into Project.

2. Double-click EvntLog.rc.

This adds the resource file to the project as well as adding the message file.

Modifying the Registry

Now that the message file has been compiled and added to the project, we write some code that creates an entry in the Registry for the Event Log, as follows:

1. Create a blank text file in Microsoft Developer Studio.

2. Add the code given in Listing 5.9 and save it as EvtLog.cpp.

3. Add the file to the project by clicking Insert | Files into Project and double-clicking EvtLog.cpp.

4. Create a definition file so that the Registry functions can be exported. Listing 5.10 shows what the definition file should look like.

5. Save the definition file as EvtLog.def.

6. Once the definition file has been saved as EvtLog.def, add it to the project by clicking Insert | Files into Project and double-clicking EvtLog.def.

7. Compile EvtLog.def by clicking Build | Build EvtLog.exe.

8. Register the executable by typing on the command line

```
regsvr32 EvntLog.dll
```

You need to be in the directory into which EvtLog.exe was built.

DllUnregisterServer is also implemented in Listing 5.9, thus allowing you to remove the Registry entries later.

Listing 5.9

```
#include <afx.h>
#include <afxext.h>               // MFC extensions
#include <afxwin.h>
#include <iostream.h>
#include <basetyps.h>

STDAPI DllRegisterServer(void)
{
DWORD dwAllocBufferLength=500;
LPTSTR  lpszBuffer=new TCHAR[dwAllocBufferLength];
HKEY   hKey=HKEY_LOCAL_MACHINE;  // handle of open key
HKEY   hkResult1;       // address of handle of open key
HKEY   hkResult2;       // address of handle of open key
DWORD ulOptions=0;
REGSAM  samDesired=KEY_ALL_ACCESS;
DWORD Reserved=0;
DWORD dwTypesSupported=7;
DWORD dwCatagoryCount=1;

// Get DLL File Location

if(!GetCurrentDirectory(dwAllocBufferLength,
lpszBuffer))
goto Error;

_tcscat(lpszBuffer,"\\EvntLog.dll");

// Event Logging Registry Settings
```

```
if (RegOpenKeyEx(hKey,"SYSTEM\\CurrentControlSet
\\Services\\EventLog\\Application",ulOptions,
samDesired,&hkResult1) !=ERROR_SUCCESS)
goto Error;

if (RegCreateKey(hkResult1,"EvntLog",&hkResult2)
!=ERROR_SUCCESS)
{
RegCloseKey(hkResult1);
goto Error;
}

if (RegSetValueEx(hkResult2,"EventMessageFile",
Reserved, REG_EXPAND_SZ,(CONST BYTE *)lpszBuffer,
_tcslen(lpszBuffer)) !=ERROR_SUCCESS)
{
RegCloseKey(hkResult1);
RegCloseKey(hkResult2);
goto Error;
}

if (RegSetValueEx(hkResult2,"CategoryMessageFile",
Reserved,REG_EXPAND_SZ,(CONST BYTE *)lpszBuffer,
_tcslen(lpszBuffer))!=ERROR_SUCCESS)
{
RegCloseKey(hkResult1);
RegCloseKey(hkResult2);
goto Error;
}

if (RegSetValueEx(hkResult2,"TypesSupported",Reserved,
REG_DWORD,(CONST BYTE *)&dwTypesSupported,
sizeof(DWORD))!=ERROR_SUCCESS)
{
RegCloseKey(hkResult1);
RegCloseKey(hkResult2);
goto Error;
}
```

```
if (RegSetValueEx(hkResult2,"CategoryCount",
Reserved,REG_DWORD,(CONST BYTE *)&dwCatagoryCount,
sizeof(DWORD))!=ERROR_SUCCESS)
{
RegCloseKey(hkResult1);
RegCloseKey(hkResult2);
goto Error;
}

RegCloseKey(hkResult1);
RegCloseKey(hkResult2);

delete lpszBuffer;

return(S_OK);

Error:
delete lpszBuffer;
return(E_UNEXPECTED);
}

STDAPI DllUnregisterServer(void)
{
if (RegDeleteKey(
HKEY_LOCAL_MACHINE,
"SYSTEM\\CurrentControlSet\\Services\\EventLog
\\Application\\EvntLog"
))
{
return (E_UNEXPECTED);
}
return (S_OK);
}
```

Registry Entries Created When EvntLog.dll Is Created

This is a good time to talk about the Registry entries that are created when you register EvntLog.dll.

To have the Event Log call your DLL, you must put an entry in the Log's Registry area. To add an application, you create a key that will hold the DLL information in HKEY_LOCAL_MACHINE\SYSTEM\ CurrentControlSet\Services\EventLog\Application\<Name>, where <Name> is the name of the application. For the example, we created HKEY_LOCAL_MACHINE\SYSTEM\CurrentControlSet\Services\ EventLog\Application\EvntLog.

At your option, you can make a subkey in the system area in HKEY_ LOCAL_MACHINE\SYSTEM\CurrentControlSet\Services\EventLog\ System and in the security area in HKEY_LOCAL_MACHINE\SYSTEM\ CurrentControlSet\Services\EventLog\Security.

The name of the key created will be the source name in the Event Log. Each key in the Registry section of the Log should have four name-value pairs regardless of whether it is under security, application, or system, as follows:

1. A DWORD called CategoryCount that holds the number of categories that the application is going to log to the Event Log. In this way, when the Log reads the message file starting at 1, it will know how many messages are categories.

2. A name-value pair called TypesSupported with a DWORD data type present in the source key that has a value of 7.

3. Two name-value pairs that point to the location of the message file. These are called EventMessageFile and CategoryMessageFile and should be of type string. If you split the message file into two DLLs, one for categories and one for messages, then you will need to assign these values accordingly. The Event Log uses these two name-value pairs to find the DLL that contains the strings to display.

Note: By translating your message DLL into other languages and shipping the correct DLL with each language, localization to the Event Log is made easy.

Logging to the Registry

To log to the Registry, you simply make the Event Log message file and modify the Registry. But the example would not be complete unless we did an example of the logging. So, next we create a console application that logs to the Registry. Follow these steps:

1. Open Microsoft Developer Studio.

2. Click File | New.

3. Click Project Workspace.

4. Name the project ELogger.

5. From the Type list, select Console Application.

6. Click Create.

7. Create a blank text file and insert the code given in Listing 5.10.

8. Save the file as Elogger.cpp and insert it into the project by clicking Insert | Files into Project and double-clicking EvtLog.cpp.

Listing 5.10

```cpp
#include <afx.h>
#include <afxext.h>              // MFC extensions
#include <afxwin.h>
#include <iostream.h>
#include <basetyps.h>

// This is the header file create by the
// Message Compiler
#include "EvntLog.h"

int main( int argc, char *argv[ ], char *envp[ ] )
{

HANDLE   hEventLog;        // handle returned by
                          // RegisterEventSource
PSID   lpUserSid=NULL;     // user security identifier
                          // (optional)
WORD   wNumStrings;        // number of strings to merge
                          // with message
DWORD dwDataSize=0;        // size of binary data, in bytes
```

```
LPTSTR  lpStrings[1];    // array of strings to merge
                         // with message
LPVOID  lpRawData=NULL;  // address of binary data

BOOL  bReturn;

// Register the Event Source So that we can write to it.

if (!(hEventLog=RegisterEventSource(NULL, "EvntLog")))
{
delete lpStrings[0];
return(1);
}

// Write an Event as a Warning

bReturn=ReportEvent(hEventLog,EVENTLOG_WARNING_TYPE,
EVCAT_TESTING,EVMSG_MEMORY1,lpUserSid,0,dwDataSize,
(LPCTSTR *) lpStrings,lpRawData);

// Write an Event as an Error

bReturn=ReportEvent(hEventLog,EVENTLOG_ERROR_TYPE,
EVCAT_TESTING,EVMSG_MEMORY1,lpUserSid,0,dwDataSize,
(LPCTSTR *) lpStrings,lpRawData);

// Create an Array of strings to write to the Event Log
// The Single String Create will be substituted for %1
// in the Message to the Event Log

wNumStrings=1;
lpStrings[0] = new TCHAR[_tcslen("Test Comment")+1];
_tcscpy(lpStrings[0],"Test Comment");

// Write an Event as Informational

bReturn=ReportEvent(hEventLog,
EVENTLOG_INFORMATION_TYPE,EVCAT_TESTING,EVMSG_MEMORY2,
```

```
lpUserSid,wNumStrings,dwDataSize,(LPCTSTR *)
lpStrings,lpRawData);

// De register the Source

if (!DeregisterEventSource(hEventLog))
{
delete lpStrings[0];
return(1);
}

delete lpStrings[0];

return(0);

}
```

Before compiling, add MFC. Follow these steps:

1. Click Build | Settings.

2. Select the General tab.

3. In the Microsoft Foundation Classes select box, select "Use MFC in a Static Library."

4. Click OK.

Next, we compile and run. When we run Elogger.exe, it will log to the Event Log. Use the Event Viewer in the Administrative Tools to view the events that are logged.

Debugging an Application That Logs to the Event Log

A common error in debugging an application that logs to the Event Log is to leave the Event Viewer open. For instance, suppose you made a spelling error in a category. In Microsoft Developer Studio, you would correct the error in the message file and then recompile the file. Once the message file was recompiled, you would recompile the DLL's resource. But when you return to the Event Viewer, the error would still show. Even if you refresh the Event Viewer, the misspelled word won't go away. The problem is, the categories load when the Event Viewer begins, so to see the change you need to close the Event Viewer and reopen it.

Logging Performance with the Performance Monitor

The Performance Monitor is a application that comes with the operating system and is used to watch the performance of applications. For an application's performance to be viewed, the application must expose APIs to the Performance Monitor and fill in a structure defined by the Monitor. The Monitor must know that the application exists, where it exists, and what the exposed APIs are. This information is available in the Registry for every application that logs to the Monitor.

The data the Monitor watches is called a **counter.** Each counter belongs to an object, and each object usually represents an application. Each counter has a unique identifier. The Monitor can follow many counters at the same time. Many different counters may be exposed from a single application, and a counter may have multiple instances. For instance, a counter that monitors CPU cycles might have an instance for every running process.

How the Registry Fits In

The Registry has a performance section for every application that wants to expose counters. Each application must have a subkey out of HKEY_LOCAL_MACHINE\SYSTEM\CurrentControlSet\Services. The subkey can be named anything, but usually it should be the name of the application. The Performance Monitor cannot view the name. For the example that follows, the subkey name of the Performance Monitor is PerfMon. There also must be a subkey out of PerfMon called Performance. All Registry settings for an application to interact with the Performance Monitor go in the Performance subkey. The full path looks like this: HKEY_LOCAL_MACHINE\SYSTEM\CurrentControlSet\Services\ PerfMon\Performance.

Generating Unique IDs

In the Performance subkey, the Performance Monitor stores the first unique ID to the counters that are in the object. From the first unique ID, all other unique IDs can be generated. To have the Performance Monitor generate a unique ID for your counter, you must run a program called lodctr.exe. For lodctr.exe to work properly, the Performance subkey must already exist. lodctr.exe generates the unique ID and creates four name-value pairs, as follows:

1. First Counter, in which it writes the first unique ID

2. First Help, which points to a unique identifier for the help string that is associated with each counter

3. Last Counter and Last Help, which contain the unique IDs of Last Counter and Last Help

lodctr.exe must know how many counters the object has and to which object the counters are associated. This information is in an .ini file, which is the only parameter to lodctr.exe. The .ini file's structure contains the name of the object, a reference to a header file, the languages the object supports, a string for every counter title, and a string for every counter explanation. The header that is referenced contains definitions for every ID. Listing 5.11 shows the structure of the .ini file.

Listing 5.11

```
[info]
drivername=PERFMON
symbolfile=genctrnm.h

[languages]
009=English

[text]
PERFMON_OBJ_009_NAME=Performance Tester
PERFMON_OBJ_009_HELP=Simulates an Application that is
Logging Performance Data
RANDOM_009_NAME=Random
RANDOM_009_HELP=A Random Number between 1-100
```

The name of the object is drivername. It must be the same as the name of the subkey out of HKEY_LOCAL_MACHINE\SYSTEM\ CurrentControlSet\Services, which is where the performance data is located. The name of the header file that contains the definitions for the IDs of each counter is symbolfile.

In the text area of the .ini file are the four strings used in the Performance Monitor to interface with users, in this order:

1. The object name

2. The explanation of that object

3. The first counter's name

4. The explanation of the name

The pattern repeats for each counter. After all the strings have been entered for the first language type, they are all repeated for the next language type, and so on, until all language types are done. Every language that the Performance Monitor understands must have an entry.

The syntax of the text names in the .ini file must be

```
<offset>_<langid>_NAME
```

where <offset> is the name of the offset from the symbol file and <langid> is the language number. The syntax of the text help in the .ini file must be

```
<offset>_<langid>_HELP
```

where <offset> is the name of the offset from the symbol file and <langid> is the language number. There must be a name and a help entry for every offset in the symbolfile and every language.

The symbol file consists of definitions. One is for the object, which is defined as 0. Also, every counter has a definition, with the first counter defined as 2 and each one after that defined incrementally by 2, for example, 4, 6, 8, and so on. Listing 5.12 shows an example symbol file.

Listing 5.12
```
//
// genctrnm.h
```

```
//
//  Offset definition file for extensible
//  counter objects and counters
//
//  These "relative" offsets must start at 0 and be
//  multiples of 2 (i.e. even numbers). In the Open
//  Procedure, they will be added to the "First
//  Counter" and "First Help" values of the device they
//  belong to, in order to determine the absolute
//  location of the counter and object names and
//  corresponding help text in the Registry.
//
//  this file is used by the extensible counter DLL
//  code as well as the counter name and help text
//  definition file (.INI) file that is used by LODCTR
//  to load the names into the Registry.
//
#define PERFMON_OBJ     0
#define RANDOM   2
```

Other Registry Settings

In addition to the Registry setting that lodctr.exe makes, the Performance Monitor needs Registry settings that tell it where the DLL is located and which APIs to use for opening the object, collecting data, and closing the object. There are four additional name-value pairs, as follows:

1. Library, located in the Performance Key, which specifies the DLL's location. This pair contains either the full path to the DLL or, if the DLL exists in the system32 directory, just the DLL's name. Our example later in the chapter creates the Library key when it is registered and inserts the full path.

2. Open, a string in the Performance key, which contains the name of the exported procedure to call when the object is opened. Its value is set to the name of the procedure.

3. Close, which tells the Performance Monitor the name of the API to call when the object is closed.

4. Collect, which tells the Performance Monitor the name of the API to call when data is being collected. Its value is the API's name.

An Example

To show you how all of the above works, we create an example that exposes APIs that the Performance Monitor can query. First, we create a DLL as follows:

1. Open Microsoft Developer Studio.

2. Click File | New.

3. Click Project Workspace.

4. Name the project PerfMon.

5. From the Type list, select Dynamic Link Library.

6. Choose the default setting.

7. Click Create.

Next, create a blank text file and insert the code shown in Listing 5.13. Then save the Listing as PerfMon.cpp.

Listing 5.13

```cpp
#include <windows.h>
#include <string.h>
#include <winperf.h>
#include <string.h>
#include "PerfMon.h"
#include "Genctrnm.h"

DWORD   dwOpenCount = 0;    // count of "Open" threads
BOOL    bInitOK = FALSE;    // true = DLL initialized OK

// DataDefinition is a global variable that holds the
// data structure that the Performance Monitor needs.
// Some of the files are calculated at compile time
// based off the size of static structures
```

```cpp
// and some of the fields are calculated when
// the OpenPerformanceData API is called.

DATA_DEFINITION DataDefinition =
{
{
sizeof(DATA_DEFINITION) + sizeof(COUNTER),
sizeof(DATA_DEFINITION),
sizeof(PERF_OBJECT_TYPE),
PERFMON_OBJ,
0,
PERFMON_OBJ,
0,
PERF_DETAIL_NOVICE,
(sizeof(DATA_DEFINITION)-sizeof(PERF_OBJECT_TYPE))/
sizeof(PERF_COUNTER_DEFINITION),
0   // assigned in Open Procedure
PERF_NO_INSTANCES,
0
}
,
// Start Section for the Random Value
// To add more Counters duplicate this section
{
sizeof(PERF_COUNTER_DEFINITION),
RANDOM, // This value is gotten from genctrnm.h
0,
RANDOM, // This value is gotten from genctrnm.h
0,
0,
PERF_DETAIL_NOVICE,
PERF_COUNTER_RAWCOUNT,
sizeof(DWORD),
0   // assigned in Open Procedure
}
// End Section for the Random Value
};
```

```
STDAPI DllRegisterServer(void)
{
DWORD dwAllocBufferLength=500;
LPTSTR  lpszBuffer= new TCHAR[dwAllocBufferLength];
HKEY  hkResult1;       // address of handle of open key
HKEY  hkResult2;       // address of handle of open key
HKEY  hkResult3;       // address of handle of open key
DWORD ulOptions=0;
REGSAM  samDesired=KEY_ALL_ACCESS;
DWORD Reserved=0;
DWORD dwTypesSupported=7;
DWORD dwCatagoryCount=1;

// Get DLL File Location

if(!GetCurrentDirectory(dwAllocBufferLength,lpszBuffer))
goto Error;

strcat(lpszBuffer,"\\perfmon.dll");

// Event Logging Registry Settings

if (RegOpenKeyEx(HKEY_LOCAL_MACHINE,
"SYSTEM\\CurrentControlSet\\Services",ulOptions,
samDesired,&hkResult1)!=ERROR_SUCCESS)
goto Error;

if (RegCreateKey(hkResult1,"PerfMon",&hkResult2)
!=ERROR_SUCCESS)
{
RegCloseKey(hkResult1);
goto Error;
}

if (RegCreateKey(hkResult2,
"Performance",&hkResult3)!=ERROR_SUCCESS)
{
RegCloseKey(hkResult1);
```

```cpp
RegCloseKey(hkResult2);
goto Error;
}

if (RegSetValueEx(hkResult3,"Library",Reserved,
REG_EXPAND_SZ,(CONST BYTE *)lpszBuffer,
strlen(lpszBuffer))!=ERROR_SUCCESS)
{
RegCloseKey(hkResult1);
RegCloseKey(hkResult2);
RegCloseKey(hkResult3);
goto Error;
}

if (RegSetValueEx(hkResult3,"Open",Reserved,REG_SZ,
(CONST BYTE *)"OpenPerformanceData",
strlen("OpenPerformanceData"))!=ERROR_SUCCESS)
{
RegCloseKey(hkResult1);
RegCloseKey(hkResult2);
RegCloseKey(hkResult3);
goto Error;
}

if (RegSetValueEx(hkResult3,"Collect",Reserved,REG_SZ,
(CONST BYTE *)"CollectPerformanceData",
strlen("CollectPerformanceData"))!=ERROR_SUCCESS)
{
RegCloseKey(hkResult1);
RegCloseKey(hkResult2);
RegCloseKey(hkResult3);
goto Error;
}

if (RegSetValueEx(hkResult3,"Close",Reserved,REG_SZ,
(CONST BYTE *)"ClosePerformanceData",
strlen("ClosePerformanceData"))!=ERROR_SUCCESS)
{
```

```c
RegCloseKey(hkResult1);
RegCloseKey(hkResult2);
RegCloseKey(hkResult3);
goto Error;
}

if (RegCloseKey(hkResult1)!=ERROR_SUCCESS)
goto Error;

if (RegCloseKey(hkResult2)!=ERROR_SUCCESS)
goto Error;

if (RegCloseKey(hkResult3)!=ERROR_SUCCESS)
goto Error;

delete lpszBuffer;

return(S_OK);

Error:
delete lpszBuffer;
return(E_UNEXPECTED);
}

STDAPI DllUnregisterServer(void)
{
if (RegDeleteKey(
HKEY_LOCAL_MACHINE,
"SYSTEM\\CurrentControlSet\\Services\\PerfMon
\\Performance"
))
{
return (E_UNEXPECTED);
}
return (S_OK);
}
```

```cpp
DWORD APIENTRY OpenPerformanceData(LPWSTR lpDeviceNames)
{
LONG    status;
HKEY    hKeyDriverPerf;
DWORD   size;
DWORD   type;
DWORD   dwFirstCounter;
DWORD   dwFirstHelp;
COUNTER ctr;

// Only do this once for this first performance
// Monitor that queries the data

if (!dwOpenCount) {

// Open the Key Created by DLLRegisterServer

status = RegOpenKeyEx (
HKEY_LOCAL_MACHINE,
"SYSTEM\\CurrentControlSet\\Services\\PerfMon
\\Performance",
0L,
KEY_READ,
&hKeyDriverPerf);

if (status != ERROR_SUCCESS)
{
goto OpenExitPoint;
}

// Get the First Counter ID
// This Registry entry got created
// by lodctr.exe

size = sizeof (DWORD);
status = RegQueryValueEx(
hKeyDriverPerf,
"First Counter",
```

```
0L,
&type,
(LPBYTE)&dwFirstCounter,
&size);

if (status != ERROR_SUCCESS)
{
goto OpenExitPoint;
}

// Get the First Help ID
// This Registry entry got created
// by lodctr.exe

size = sizeof (DWORD);
status = RegQueryValueEx(
hKeyDriverPerf,
"First Help",
0L,
&type,
(LPBYTE)&dwFirstHelp,
&size);

if (status != ERROR_SUCCESS)
{
goto OpenExitPoint;
}

DataDefinition.ObjectType.ObjectNameTitleIndex +=
dwFirstCounter;
DataDefinition.ObjectType.ObjectHelpTitleIndex +=
dwFirstHelp;

// assign index of default counter
DataDefinition.ObjectType.DefaultCounter = 0;

// This is the Section for the Random Value
// Repeat this section for extra Counters
```

```
DataDefinition.Random.CounterNameTitleIndex +=
dwFirstCounter;
DataDefinition.Random.CounterHelpTitleIndex +=
dwFirstHelp;
DataDefinition.Random.CounterOffset =
(DWORD)((LPBYTE)(&ctr.dwRandomValue) - (LPBYTE)&ctr);

// This is to seed the random value we are going to use
// for Make believe performance data

SYSTEMTIME  st;
GetSystemTime (&st);
srand(st.wMilliseconds);

bInitOK = TRUE; // ok to use this function
}

dwOpenCount++;  // increment OPEN counter

status = ERROR_SUCCESS; // for successful exit

OpenExitPoint:

return status;
}


DWORD APIENTRY CollectPerformanceData(
IN      LPWSTR  lpValueName,
IN OUT  LPVOID  *lppData,
IN OUT  LPDWORD lpcbTotalBytes,
IN OUT  LPDWORD lpNumObjectTypes
)
{

PERF_INSTANCE_DEFINITION  *pPerfInstanceDefinition;
DWORD             dwThisInstance;
ULONG             SpaceNeeded;
```

```
DATA_DEFINITION        *pDataDefinition;
DWORD           dwQueryType;
COUNTER            *pSC;

// Check to make sure that we opened OK.

if (!bInitOK)
{
// unable to continue because open failed.
*lpcbTotalBytes = (DWORD) 0;
*lpNumObjectTypes = (DWORD) 0;
return ERROR_SUCCESS; // yes, this is a successful exit
}

dwQueryType = GetQueryType (lpValueName);

// Exit on Foreign requests, Non NT.
if (dwQueryType == QUERY_FOREIGN)
{
*lpcbTotalBytes = (DWORD) 0;
*lpNumObjectTypes = (DWORD) 0;
return ERROR_SUCCESS;
}


if (dwQueryType == QUERY_ITEMS)
{
// The Item request can't be handled
if ( !(IsNumberInUnicodeList
(DataDefinition.ObjectType.ObjectNameTitleIndex,
lpValueName))) {
*lpcbTotalBytes = (DWORD) 0;
*lpNumObjectTypes = (DWORD) 0;
return ERROR_SUCCESS;
}
}

pDataDefinition = (DATA_DEFINITION *) *lppData;
```

```
SpaceNeeded = sizeof(DATA_DEFINITION) +
(NUM_INSTANCES * (sizeof(PERF_INSTANCE_DEFINITION) +
(sizeof(wdInstance[0].szInstanceName)) +  // size of
                                          // instance names
sizeof (COUNTER)));

if ( *lpcbTotalBytes < SpaceNeeded )
{
*lpcbTotalBytes = (DWORD) 0;
*lpNumObjectTypes = (DWORD) 0;
return ERROR_MORE_DATA;
}

//
// Copy the (constant, initialized) Object Type and
// counter definitions to the caller's data buffer
//

memmove(pDataDefinition,
&DataDefinition,
sizeof(DATA_DEFINITION));

//  Create data for return for each instance

pPerfInstanceDefinition = (PERF_INSTANCE_DEFINITION *)
&pDataDefinition[1];

for (dwThisInstance = 0; dwThisInstance < NUM_INSTANCES;
dwThisInstance++)
{

BuildInstanceDefinition(
pPerfInstanceDefinition,
(PVOID *)&pSC,
0,
0,
(DWORD)-1, // use name
wdInstance[dwThisInstance].szInstanceName);
```

```c
pSC->CounterBlock.ByteLength = sizeof (COUNTER);

// The Example Sends back a random number, usually
// you would send back variables that
// show the performance hit.

int dwRandom=rand();
dwRandom=dwRandom*((double)100.0/(double)RAND_MAX);
pSC->dwRandomValue = (DWORD)dwRandom;

// update instance pointer for next instance
pPerfInstanceDefinition = (PERF_INSTANCE_DEFINITION *)
&pSC[1];
}
// update arguments for return

*lppData = (PVOID)pPerfInstanceDefinition;

*lpNumObjectTypes = 1;

pDataDefinition->ObjectType.TotalByteLength =
*lpcbTotalBytes = (PBYTE)pPerfInstanceDefinition -
(PBYTE) pDataDefinition;

// update instance count
pDataDefinition->ObjectType.NumInstances =
NUM_INSTANCES;

return ERROR_SUCCESS;
}

BOOL IsNumberInUnicodeList (
IN DWORD    dwNumber,
IN LPWSTR   lpwszUnicodeList
)
{
DWORD    dwThisNumber;
WCHAR    *pwcThisChar;
```

```
BOOL    bValidNumber;
BOOL    bNewItem;
WCHAR   wcDelimiter;   // could be an argument to be
                       // more flexible

if (lpwszUnicodeList == 0) return FALSE; // null
                                  // pointer, # not found

pwcThisChar = lpwszUnicodeList;
dwThisNumber = 0;
wcDelimiter = (WCHAR)' ';
bValidNumber = FALSE;
bNewItem = TRUE;

while (TRUE) {
switch (EvalThisChar (*pwcThisChar, wcDelimiter)) {
case DIGIT:
// if this is the first digit after a delimiter, then
// set flags to start computing the new number
if (bNewItem) {
bNewItem = FALSE;
bValidNumber = TRUE;
}
if (bValidNumber) {
dwThisNumber *= 10;
dwThisNumber += (*pwcThisChar - (WCHAR)'0');
}
break;

case DELIMITER:
// a delimiter is either the delimiter character or the
// end of the string ('\0') if when the delimiter has
// been reached a valid number was found, then compare
// it to the number from the argument list. if this is
// the end of the string and no match was found, then
// return.
//
```

```
if (bValidNumber) {
if (dwThisNumber == dwNumber) return TRUE;
bValidNumber = FALSE;
}
if (*pwcThisChar == 0) {
return FALSE;
} else {
bNewItem = TRUE;
dwThisNumber = 0;
}
break;

case INVALID:
// if an invalid character was encountered, ignore all
// characters up to the next delimiter and then start
// fresh. the invalid number is not compared.
bValidNumber = FALSE;
break;

default:
break;

}
pwcThisChar++;
}
return FALSE;
}    // IsNumberInUnicodeList

BOOL BuildInstanceDefinition(
PERF_INSTANCE_DEFINITION *pBuffer,
PVOID *pBufferNext,
DWORD ParentObjectTitleIndex,
DWORD ParentObjectInstance,
DWORD UniqueID,
LPWSTR Name
)
{
DWORD NameLength;
```

```
LPWSTR pName;
//
//   Include trailing null in name size
//

NameLength = (lstrlenW(Name) + 1) * sizeof(WCHAR);

pBuffer->ByteLength = sizeof(PERF_INSTANCE_DEFINITION)
+ DWORD_MULTIPLE(NameLength);

pBuffer->ParentObjectTitleIndex =
ParentObjectTitleIndex;
pBuffer->ParentObjectInstance = ParentObjectInstance;
pBuffer->UniqueID = UniqueID;
pBuffer->NameOffset = sizeof(PERF_INSTANCE_DEFINITION);
pBuffer->NameLength = NameLength;

// copy name to name buffer
pName = (LPWSTR)&pBuffer[1];
RtlMoveMemory(pName,Name,NameLength);

// update "next byte" pointer
*pBufferNext = (PVOID) ((PCHAR) pBuffer + pBuffer->
ByteLength);

return 0;
}

DWORD GetQueryType (IN LPWSTR lpValue)
/*++

GetQueryType

returns the type of query described in the lpValue
string so that the appropriate processing method may be
used

Arguments
```

```
IN lpValue
string passed to PerfRegQuery Value for processing

Return Value

QUERY_GLOBAL
if lpValue == 0 (null pointer)
lpValue == pointer to Null string
lpValue == pointer to "Global" string

QUERY_FOREIGN
if lpValue == pointer to "Foreign" string
QUERY_COSTLY
if lpValue == pointer to "Costly" string

otherwise:

QUERY_ITEMS

--*/
{
WCHAR    *pwcArgChar, *pwcTypeChar;
BOOL     bFound;

if (lpValue == 0) {
return QUERY_GLOBAL;
} else if (*lpValue == 0) {
return QUERY_GLOBAL;
}

// check for "Global" request

pwcArgChar = lpValue;
pwcTypeChar = GLOBAL_STRING;
bFound = TRUE;  // assume found until contradicted

// check to the length of the shortest string
```

```cpp
while ((*pwcArgChar != 0) && (*pwcTypeChar != 0)) {
if (*pwcArgChar++ != *pwcTypeChar++) {
bFound = FALSE; // no match
break;          // bail out now
}
}

if (bFound) return QUERY_GLOBAL;

// check for "Foreign" request

pwcArgChar = lpValue;
pwcTypeChar = FOREIGN_STRING;
bFound = TRUE;  // assume found until contradicted

// check to the length of the shortest string

while ((*pwcArgChar != 0) && (*pwcTypeChar != 0)) {
if (*pwcArgChar++ != *pwcTypeChar++) {
bFound = FALSE; // no match
break;          // bail out now
}
}

if (bFound) return QUERY_FOREIGN;

// check for "Costly" request

pwcArgChar = lpValue;
pwcTypeChar = COSTLY_STRING;
bFound = TRUE;  // assume found until contradicted

// check to the length of the shortest string

while ((*pwcArgChar != 0) && (*pwcTypeChar != 0)) {
if (*pwcArgChar++ != *pwcTypeChar++) {
bFound = FALSE; // no match
break;          // bail out now
```

```
}
}

if (bFound) return QUERY_COSTLY;

// if not Global and not Foreign and not Costly,
// then it must be an item list

return QUERY_ITEMS;

}

DWORD APIENTRY ClosePerformanceData()
{
dwOpenCount--;
return ERROR_SUCCESS;
}
```

Then we create another blank text file and insert the header for
PerfMon.cpp from the code in Listing 5.14. We save the Listing as
PerfMon.cpp.

Listing 5.14

```
//PerfMon.h

#define QUERY_GLOBAL     1
#define QUERY_ITEMS      2
#define QUERY_FOREIGN    3
#define QUERY_COSTLY     4

// test for delimiter, end of line and non-digit
// characters used by IsNumberInUnicodeList routine
//
#define DIGIT         1
#define DELIMITER     2
#define INVALID       3
```

```cpp
WCHAR GLOBAL_STRING[] = L"Global";
WCHAR FOREIGN_STRING[] = L"Foreign";
WCHAR COSTLY_STRING[] = L"Costly";

#define EvalThisChar(c,d) ( \
(c == d) ? DELIMITER : \
(c == 0) ? DELIMITER : \
(c < (WCHAR)'0') ? INVALID : \
(c > (WCHAR)'9') ? INVALID : \
DIGIT)

typedef struct
{
PERF_OBJECT_TYPE     ObjectType;
PERF_COUNTER_DEFINITION Random;
} DATA_DEFINITION;

typedef struct
{
PERF_COUNTER_BLOCK        CounterBlock;
// There is only one Value that is Random
// To Add more values add them here.
DWORD                    dwRandomValue;
} COUNTER, far * LPCOUNTER;

// These are the declarations for the
// Exposed Performance APIS

PM_OPEN_PROC     OpenPerformanceData;
PM_COLLECT_PROC CollectPerformanceData;
PM_CLOSE_PROC    ClosePerformanceData;

// There many be many instances of each counter
// This routine builds the instances when
// a collect is called.
BOOL BuildInstanceDefinition(
PERF_INSTANCE_DEFINITION *pBuffer,
PVOID *pBufferNext,
```

```c
DWORD ParentObjectTitleIndex,
DWORD ParentObjectInstance,
DWORD UniqueID,
LPWSTR Name
);

BOOL IsNumberInUnicodeList (
IN DWORD    dwNumber,
IN LPWSTR   lpwszUnicodeList
);

DWORD GetQueryType (IN LPWSTR lpValue);

// This is the structure which contains
// The attributes of an Instance
// Since there are no attributes to
// a random number there is only the
// Instances Name

// To add attributes put them
// in this data structure
typedef struct
{
LPWSTR   szInstanceName;
} INSTANCE_DATE, *PINSTANCE_DATE;

// To fill in attributes of each instance
// fill out this static data.
// If the attribute is dynamic based on
// a runtime calculation then
// fill the data structure in
// in the OpenPerformaceData API

// Since a Random Number has no
// Attributes then there is only
// The title to fill out.
```

```
static INSTANCE_DATE wdInstance[]   =
{
{L"Random #1"},
{L"Random #2"},
};

// Calculate the Number of Instances based
// on the size of wdInstancs

static const DWORD    NUM_INSTANCES =
(sizeof(wdInstance)/sizeof(wdInstance[0]));

#define DWORD_MULTIPLE(x) (((x+sizeof(DWORD)-1)/
sizeof(DWORD))*sizeof(DWORD))
```

Next, we do the following:

1. Create another blank text file and insert Listing 5.11. We save this file as perfmon.ini.

2. Create another blank text file and insert the code from Listing 5.12. We save this file as Genctrnm.h.

3. Create a final blank file and insert the code given in Listing 5.15. We save the Listing as PerfMon.cpp.

Listing 5.15

```
LIBRARY PerfMon

DESCRIPTION 'PerfMon'

EXPORTS
OpenPerformanceData      @1
CollectPerformanceData   @2
ClosePerformanceData     @3
DllRegisterServer        @4
DllUnregisterServer      @5
```

Now we add PerfMon.cpp and PerfMon.def to the project by following these steps:

1. Click Insert | Files into Project.

2. Double-click PerfMon.cpp.

3. Double-click PerfMon.def.

Finally, we compile the example. Once it is compiled, we should have a DLL named PerfMon.dll.

Running the Example

To run the example, we first register the DLL and then run lodctr.exe. Register the DLL as follows:

1. Open a DOS box and go to the directory that holds the DLL.

2. Type

```
regsvr32 PerfMon.dll
```

3. Create the Performance key for PerfMon by typing HKEY_LOCAL_ MACHINE\SYSTEM\CurrentControlSet\Services\PerfMon\ Performance.

   This also will create the name-value pairs Library, Open, Collect, and Close. Open the Registry Editor in order to view the name-value pairs.

Next, we run lodctr.exe. However, first you must register the DLL, since lodctr needs the PerfMon/Performance key. In the directory where both perfmon.ini and Genctrnm.h are located, type

```
lodctr perfmon.ini
```

This will create in the Performance key the name-value pairs First Counter, Last Counter, First Help, and Last Help.

Warning: Do not run lodctr.exe more than once. If you do, it will allocate another set of unique counter IDs.

To remove the object and its counter created in the example, follow the instructions in the last section in the chapter, Removing the Example.

After registering the DLL and running lodctr.exe, test the example as follows:

1. Open the Performance Monitor.

2. Select Edit | Add to Chart.

3. From the Object list, select Performance Tester and from the Counter list, select Random. A randomly numbered counter appears in the Performance Monitor.

Debugging the Example

To debug the example, use the Performance Monitor as the executable. Follow these steps:

1. Open Microsoft Developer Studio.

2. Load the project that contains the PerfMon example.

3. Choose Build | Setting.

4. Click the Debug tab.

5. In the "Executable for debug session" edit box, enter

   ```
   c:\winnt\system32\perfmon.exe
   ```

   Note to Windows 95 users: You need to type in the correct path to perfmon.exe.

6. Click OK.

Now you can execute the Performance Monitor in Microsoft Developer Studio and debug perfmon.dll.

Removing the Example

Here's how to remove the example:

1. Close the Performance Monitor.

2. Run unlodctr.exe to remove the unique counter IDs associated with the counters. Unlodctr.exe takes one parameter: the name of the .ini file that was used when lodctr.exe was run; for example, unlodctr.exe perfmon.ini.

Warning: To remove the example correctly, you must use the same .ini file with no modifications. Once unlodctr.exe is run, unregister the DLL by typing this command line:

```
regsvr32 /u perfmon.dll
```

Chapter 6

ActiveX Technology Support within the Registry

All Microsoft Internet solution technologies are a subset of the broader Microsoft ActiveX technology. The ActiveX technology encompasses many subtechnologies: ActiveX Controls, ActiveX Scripting, Active Document, and ActiveX Server Framework. The infrastructure of ActiveX relies exclusively on the Registry to store and maintain all the information needed to support each subtechnology.

In this chapter, we present an overview of ActiveX and the Registry keys that are predefined by OLE (Object Linking and Embedding) and the Microsoft Internet Information Server.

Overview of ActiveX

ActiveX exposes a powerful set of APIs that enables a developer to take advantage of new-generation client/server applications for the Internet. It has many interfaces that support the seamless use of almost every media technology. It also provides extensive support for animation, 3D virtual reality, real-time audio, and real-time video. Large improvements in synchronizing concurrent media streams is also inherent when using ActiveX controls.

ActiveX provides developers with an open framework for building innovative applications for the Internet. Its technologies form a robust framework for creating interactive content using software components, scripts, and applications. ActiveX technologies enable content providers and Internet application developers to create dynamic Web content and Web server extensions more easily than ever imagined. ActiveX controls, active scripts, and the active document interfaces expose a rich set of features that allow developers of all levels to be creative in never thought of ways. Through ActiveX Scripting, the developers can use Visual Basic Scripting to trigger execution and usage of all ActiveX technologies.

Microsoft ActiveX Scripting also provides an infrastructure that allows developers to use any scripting engine within Microsoft Internet Explorer 3.0 (IE 3.0). Two of the common scripting engines are VBScript and JavaScript. IE 3.0 is implemented as an OLE automation server, OLE control, Document Object Container, and a script engine host. A vender can build a custom script engine by implementing the set of interfaces required for a script engine.

ActiveX controls are formerly known as OLE controls. ActiveX controls are based on the Component Object Model (COM). The internals of COM depend on the Registry for its predefined keys, values, and the Registry information storage protocol. When an application uses an ActiveX control, it creates an instance of the control by using either the control's CLSID or ProgID. These IDs are stored in the Registry. Figure 6.1 illustrates how the Registry is involved in the instantiation of a MAPI Folder ActiveX control.

Before an ActiveX control can be used, it must be registered in the system Registry. COM defines all OLE application-related information under the predefined HKEY_CLASSES_ROOT key. COM also uses this information to locate objects and to determine the capability provided by the ActiveX controls registered on the system.

There are two ways to register ActiveX control. One way is to create a registration file and use the regedit utility to insert the information in the file into the Registry. The following command inserts the file xxx.reg into the Registry:

```
Regedit /s xxx.reg
```

Note: The /s switch will cause the information to be written into the system Registry in silent mode.

The other way to insert the data into the Registry is to provide the self-registering capability by exporting some predefined DLL entry points or to

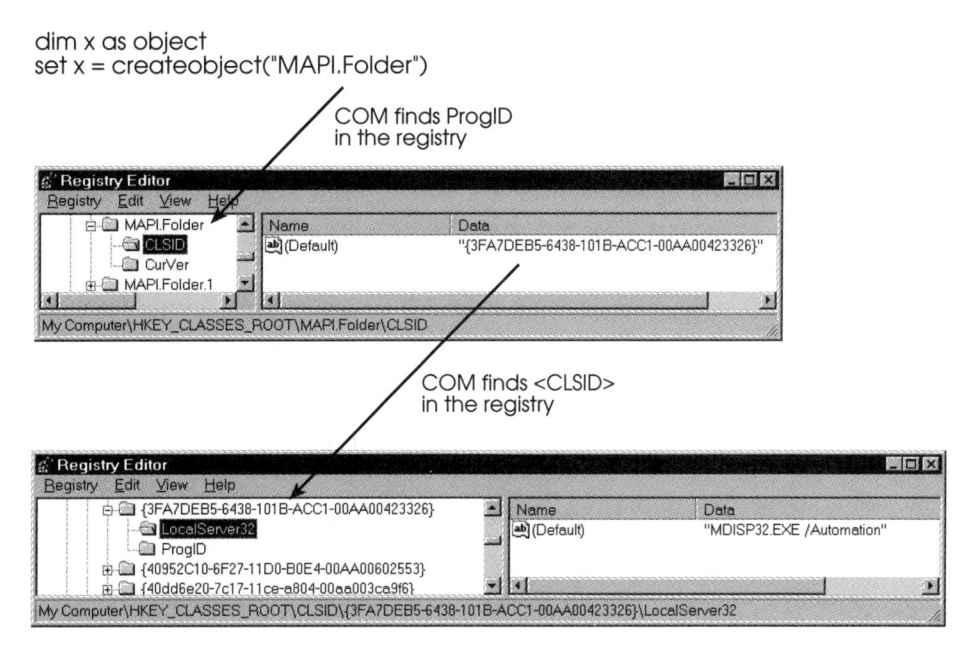

Figure 6.1 Registry and ActiveX control instantiation

accept some predefined program arguments. Chapter 5 explains how to self-register a DLL or EXE.

In the next section, we describe the Registry entries that pertain to the registration of an OLE application.

OLE Applications Registry Entries

In this section, we describe the Registry entries for OLE applications. There are five primary keys:

1. CLSID

2. ProfID

3. TypeLib

4. Interface

5. AppID

Each primary key also has many subkeys. All of these are discussed in the following sections. By the time you reach the end, you should have a good idea of how crucial the Registry is in supporting Microsoft ActiveX technology.

A particular notation is used here to interpret the hierarchy of the keys and subkeys. For example, key Server, shown next, uses an indented notation to show a hierarchy of keys that contains other keys, or subkeys:

Server = <full path to the server object>

Verb //verb is a subkey of server.

0 = < verb 0> //0 is a subkey of Verb.

1 = <verb 1> //1 is a subkey of Verb.

Here, <full path to the server object> is the value data of the key Server. The value type for <full path to the server object> is REG_SZ. There is no value name associated with it (value name is NONE).

CLSID Key

The HKEY_CLASSES_ROOT\CLSID key contains entries for each OLE application installed on your machine. The CLSID is used by OLE to identify the objects and features that are supported by the object that has the CLSID. Each OLE application has its own CLSID. A CLSID is a universally unique identifier (UUID) and is 16 bytes long. The structure of the UUID is defined as follows:

```
typedef struct tagUUID {
unsigned long Data1;
unsigned short Data2;
unsigned short Data3;
unsigned char Data4[8];
}   UUID;
```

Each OLE application's CLSID is stored in a string format of a UUID. The string representation of the CLSID, <CLSID>, is represented by a string consisting of eight hexadecimal digits followed by a hyphen and then three groups of four hexadecimal digits, each followed by a hyphen, and then finally by 12 hexadecimal digits. For example, A38D29C2-6A4F-11d0-B0DC-00AA00602553 is a string representation of the CLSID.

Each <CLSID> entry has several subkeys that store information specific to the object. Following are descriptions of the possible subkeys. The keys are case insensitive; the information in the name-value pair is case sensitive.

LocalServer Key

HKEY_CLASSES_ROOT\CLSID\<CLISD>\LocalServer = <full path to the object's 16 bit executable>

This key indicates that the object is a 16-bit out-of-process server. The value data is the full path to the object's 16-bit executable.

LocalServer32 Key

HKEY_CLASSES_ROOT\CLSID\<CLSID>\LocalServer32 = <full path to the object's 32-bit executable>

This key indicates that the object is a 32-bit out-of-process server. There are two types of COM server: local and in-process. *Local server* means the COM server runs in its own process space. *In-process server* means the COM server runs in the same process space as the application that uses the COM server.

InprocServer Key

HKEY_CLASSES_ROOT\CLSID\<CLSID>\InprocServer = <full path to the object's 16-bit DLL>

This key indicates that the object is a 16-bit in-process server. This following optional name-value pair indicates that the threading model is supported by the server:

Name: ThreadingModel

Value: "Apartment" or "Both"

"Both" specifies that the threading model is both apartment and free threading.

InprocServer32 Key

HKEY_CLASSES_ROOT\CLSID\<CLSID>\InprocServer32 = <full path to the object's 32 bit DLL>

This key indicates that the object is a 32-bit in-process server. The optional name-value pair indicates that the threading model is supported by this server:

Name: ThreadingModel

Value: "Apartment" or "Both"

"Both" indicates that the threading model is both apartment and free threading.

Insertable Key

HKEY_CLASSES_ROOT\CLSID\<CLSID>\ Insertable

This key indicates that the object can be embedded in an OLE 2.0 container application. It also appears under the ProgID key if it is present under the <CLSID>.

ProgID Key

HKEY_CLASSES_ROOT\CLSID\<CLSID>\ ProgID =< programmatic identifier>

The ProgID represents the programmatic identifier, which is stored as a string.

Note: This string must start with a digit. It also must be fewer than 39 characters and cannot contain any punctuation or underscores. It can include from one to many periods.

The naming convention for the ProgID is usually AppName.ObjectName. VersionNumber where VersionNumber is optional.

There are two kinds of ProgID. One depends on the version; the other does not. If VersionNumber is present, then the ProgID is version-dependent. Otherwise, it is version-independent. See, for example, the Word.Document ProgID in Figure 6.2.

For key Word.Document in Figure 6.2, the application name is Word and the object name is Document. For key Word.Document.6 in Figure 6.2, 6 is the version number.

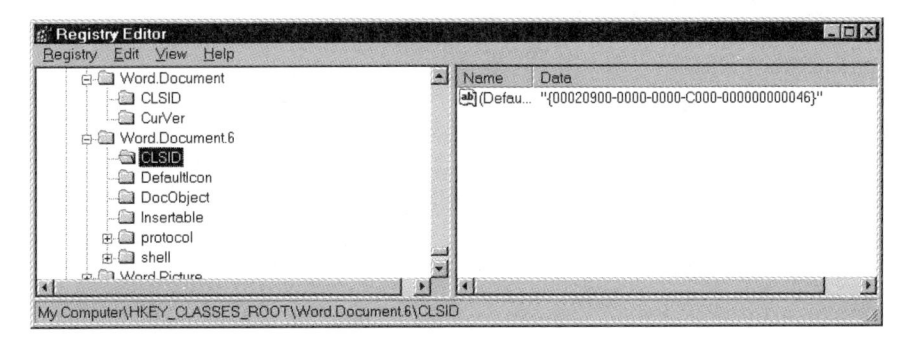

Figure 6.2 Word.Document ProgID

A version-independent ProgID can be used when a container application wants to use the most recent version of the object application. A version-dependent ProgID is used when OLE 1.0 is trying to interact with OLE 2.0 by using Dynamic Data Exchange.

Control Key

HKEY_CLASSES_ROOT\CLSID\<CLSID>\ Control
The presence of this key indicates that the object is an OLE custom control.

If you create a custom control using the Visual C++ Control Wizard, this key will be created for you.

To enumerate all controls registered on your system, enumerate every <CLSID> under HKEY_CLASSES_ROOT\CLSID and then check whether the Control key is present under the <CLSID>.

OLEScript Key

HKEY_CLASSES_ROOT\CLSID\<CLSID>\ OLEScript
If present, this key identifies the object as a scripting engine. For example, this key is present for the scripting engines VBScript and JavaScript. In Figure 6.3, OLEScript key is present in the VBScript engine.

DocObject Key

HKEY_CLASSES_ROOT\CLSID\<CLSID>\DocObject
When present, this key identifies the object as a document object. For example, this key is present for Microsoft Word, since Word is a document

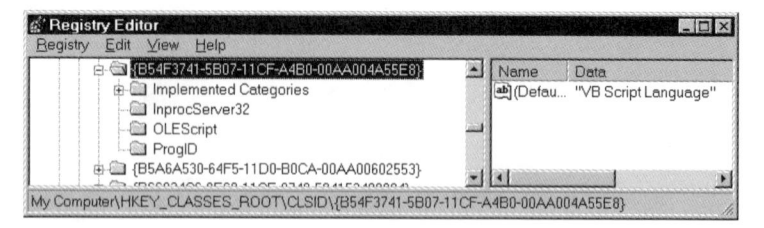

Figure 6.3 OLEScript key in VBScript engine

object. Other document objects include the applications Microsoft Excel and Visio.

Printable Key

HKEY_CLASSES_ROOT\CLSID\<CLSID>\Printable
The presence of this key indicates that the object is printable.

DefaultIcon Key

HKEY_CLASSES_ROOT\CLSID\<CLSID>\DefaultIcon = <full path to exe, index>
This key specifies the object's default icon. For example, the DefaultIcon entry for Microsoft Word on our machine is

```
D:\word\Winword\WINWORD.EXE,0
```

DefaultExtension Key

HKEY_CLASSES_ROOT\CLSID\<CLSID>\DefaultExtension
This key specifies the extension used by the object's file. It is required for any document object. For example, the default extension used by the Word document file is .doc.

MiscStatus Key

HKEY_CLASSES_ROOT\CLSID\<CLSID>\MiscStatus = <default status used for all aspects>
This key can contain the following subkey:

<aspect> = <misc status bit>

where <aspect> is an integer that can be any value defined in the tagDVASPECT. It is a desired data or view aspect of the object.

```
typedef enum tagDVASPECT
{
DVASPECT_CONTENT = 1, // the object can be displayed
// as an embedded object inside a container
DVASPECT_THUMBNAIL = 2, // the object can be
// displayed in a browsing tool
DVASEPCT_ICON = 4, // an iconic representation of an
// object
DVASPECT_DOCPRINT = 8  // the object can be
// represented on the screen
}
```

<misc status bit> is used by the container application to obtain the contained application's capabilities without creating an instance of the object.

The possible value for <misc status bit> can be any values defined in the enumeration data type tagOLEMISC, listed as follows:

```
typedef enum tagOLEMISC
{
OLEMISC_RECOMPOSERESIZE = 1, // The object
// recomposes the representation when the container
// resizes.
OLEMISC_ONLYICONIC = 2, // The object has no useful
// content view except an icon.
OLEMISC_INSERTNOTREPLACE = 4, // The object has
// initialized itself from the data in the
// container's current selection.
OLEMISC_STATIC = 8, // The object is a static
// object.
OLEMISC_CANTLINKINSIDE = 16, // The object cannot be
// the link source.
OLEMISC_CANLINKBYOLE1 = 32, // The object can be
// linked by an OLE 1 container.
OLEMISC_ISLINKOBJECT = 64, // The object is a link
// object.
```

```
OLEMISC_INSIDEOUT= 128, // The object can be
// activated in-place.
OLEMISC_ACTIVATEWHENVISIBLE = 256, // The object is
// activated when is visible.
OLEMISC_RENDERINGISDEVICEINDEPENDENT = 512, // Target
// devices are not considered.
OLEMISC_INVISIBLETRUNTIME = 1024, // The control has
// no runtime user interface. This misc status is
// for control only.
OLEMISC_ALWAYSRUN = 2048, // The control wants to be
// running. This misc status is for control only.
OLEMISC_ACTSLIKEBUTTON = 4096, // The control is
// like a button, which means it can understand the
// container's DisplayAsDefault ambient property.
// This misc status is for control only.
OLEMISC_ACTSLIKELABEL = 8192, // The control is like
// a label. This misc status is for control only.
OLEMISC_NOUIACTIVATE = 16384, // The control does
// not have UI active state. This misc status is for
// control only.
OLEMISC_ALIGNABLE = 32768, // The control can align
// itself within its display rectangle according to
// alignment properties such as left, center, and
// right.
OLEMISC_SIMPLEFRAME = 65536, // The control is a
// group of other controls and does little more than
// pass windows' messages to the control container
// managing the form.
OLEMISC_SETCLIENTSITEFIRST = 120172, // The control
// uses IOleObject::SetClientSite as its
// initialization function.
OLEMSIC_IMEMODE = 242144, // The control is an Input
// Method Editor(IME). You can use an IME to enter
// information in large Asian character set with a
// regular keyboard.
} OLEMISC;
```

Verb Key

HKEY_CLASSES_ROOT\CLSID\<CLSID>\Verb

The default handler implementation of the IOleObject::EnumVerbs uses this Registry entry to enumerate an object's verbs. The verb indicates the behavior of an embedded item in OLE activation. The Verb key can contain the following subkey:

<verb number> = <name, menu flags, verb flags>

The subkey <verb number> is an integer.

Note: The verbs for OLE objects must be numbered consecutively.

AuxUserType Key

HKEY_CLASSES_ROOT\CLSID\<CLSID>\AuxUserType

This key can contain subkeys in this format:

<form of type> = <string>

The information stored in these subkeys describes the short and long forms of human-readable names of the application. The short name is used in menus. The long name contains the actual name of the application and is used in the Paste special dialog box.

The method IOleObject::GetUserType returns this human-readable string by specifying a value that describes the form of the string to be returned. The possible values that can be returned are defined as follows in the USERCLASSTYPE enumeration:

```
typedef enum tagUSERCLASSTYPE {
USERCLASSTYPE_FULL    = 1,
USERCLASSTYPE_SHORT   = 2,
USERCLASSTYPE_APPNAME = 3,
} USERCLASSTYPE;
```

TreatAs Key

HKEY_CLASSES_ROOT\CLSID\<CLSID>\TreatAs = <CLSID>

This key is the CLSID of a registered object that can emulate the object in question (if any). It is set by an object through a call to the CoTreatAsClass function.

223

DataFormats Key

HKEY_CLASSES_ROOT\CLSID\<CLSID>\DataFormats
This key can contain the following subkeys:

DefaultFile = <format> // default main file/object format of objects
of this class **GetSet**

<n> = <format, aspect, medium, flag>

For <n> = <format, aspect, medium, flag>, the following is true:

■ *<n>* is a zero-based integer index.

■ *format* refers to Clipboard format.

■ *aspect* is one or more DVASPECT values; –1 for "all" options in
DVASPECT.

■ *medium* is one or more of the TYPMDED values.

■ *flag* is one or more of DATADIR values.

The TYPMDED enumeration values are used in the STGMEDIUM or
FORMATETC structure to indicate the type of storage medium being used
in the data transfer. The enumeration value for TYPMDED is defined as
follows:

```
typedef enum tagTYMED
{
TYMED_HGLOBAL = 1,  //global memory handle
TYMED_FILE = 2,  //a disk file identified by a path
TYMED_ISTREAM = 4,  //stream object identified by an
// Istream pointer
TYMED_ISTORAGE = 8,  //storage component identified
by an Istorage pointer
TYMED_GDI = 16,  //GDI component (HBITMAP)
TYMED_MFPICT = 32,  //metafile
TYMED_ENHMF = 64,  //enhanced metafile
TYMED_NULL = 0   //no data is being passed
}TYMED;
```

The DATADIR enumeration value is used by the container application to check the kind of get/set that is supported by the contained application.

```
Typedef enum tagDATADIR
{
DATADIR_GET = 1,
DATADIR_SET = 2
}DATADIR;
```

Interfaces Key

HKEY_CLASSES_ROOT\CLSID\<CLSID>\Interfaces =< IID, IID, …>
IID is the string representation of the interface ID. The value of the Interfaces key lists the interfaces supported by the class that is associated with the particular CLSID.

Conversion Key

HKEY_CLASSES_ROOT\CLSID\<CLSID>\Conversion
This key stores the formats that the application can read from and write to. It is used to support the Change Type dialog box. It can contain the following subkeys:

Readable (subkey)

Main = <format, format, …>

ReadWritable (subkey)

Main = <format, format, …>

Readable indicates a file format that the application can convert from (read). ReadWritable indicates a file format that the application can read from and write to.

VersionIndependentProgID Key

HKEY_CLASSES_ROOT\CLSID\<CLSID>\VersionIndependentProgID= <Version Independent ProgID>
This key stores the name of the object application's latest version. Two subkeys are currently supported:

CLSID = <CLSID>

CurVer = <ProgID>

<CLSID> is the class ID of the latest installed version of the object application. ProgID> is the ProgID of the latest installed version of the object application.

Programmable Key

HKEY_CLASSES_ROOT\CLSID\<CLSID>\Programmable
This key indicates that the object is an OLE automation server. If you want to enumerate all the OLE automation servers registered on your machine, enumerate every <CLSID> and check whether there is a programmable key present under <CLSID>.

Implemented Categories Key

HKEY_CLASSES_ROOT\CLSID\<CLSID>\Implemented Categories
This key categorizes all types of COM objects. It contains the subkeys shown in Table 6.1.

Table 6.1 Implemented Categories subkeys

Subkey	Meaning
40FC6ED3-2438-11CF-A3DB-080036F12502	An OLE embeddable object.
40FC6ED4-2438-11CF-A3DB-080036F12502	OLE control.
40FC6ED5-2438-11CF-A3DB-080036F12502	OLE automation object.
40FC6ED8-2438-11CF-A3DB-080036F12502	OLE document object.
40FC6ED9-2438-11CF-A3DB-080036F12502	Printable.
7DD95801-9882-11CF-9FA9-00AA006C42C4	A control that is safely scriptable.
7DD95802-9882-11CF-9FA9-00AA006C42C4	A control that can safely be initialized from persistent data.
F0B7A1A1-9847-11CF-8F20-00805F2CD064	Active Scripting Engine.
F0B7A1A2-9847-11CF-8F20-00805F2CD064	Active Scripting Engine with parsing.

ToolboxBitmap32 Key

HKEY_CLASSES_ROOT\CLSID\<CLSID>\ToolboxBitmap32 = <full path to the control>

This key specifies the absolute, or full, path of the control's location.

TypeLib Key

HKEY_CLASSES_ROOT\CLSID\<CLSID>\TypeLib=<TYPELIB>

This key specifies the corresponding <TYPELIB> for the given <CLSID>. <TYPELIB> is the string representation of the type library identifier, which is a UUID.

Version Key

HKEY_CLASSES_ROOT\CLSID\<CLSID>\Version=<version number>

This key specifies the version number of the OLE application.

InProcHandler Key

HKEY_CLASSES_ROOT\CLSID\<CLSID>\InProcHandler=
<in proc handler>

This key specifies whether the application uses a custom handler. If no custom handler is used, the entry should be set to OLE2.DLL.

InprocHandler32

HKEY_CLASSES_ROOT\CLSID\<CLSID>\InProcHandler32=
<in proc handler>

This key specifies whether the application uses a custom handler.

AppID Key

HKEY_CLASSES_ROOT\CLSID\<CLSID>\AppID=<AppID>

This key specifies the corresponding <APPID> for the given <CLSID>. <APPID> stands for the string representation of the application identifier, which is a UUID.

Ole1Class Key

HKEY_CLASSES_ROOT\CLSID\<CLSID>\Ole1Class

This key identifies the object as an OLE 1.0 object.

ProgID Key and Its Subkeys

The ProgID key stores the human-readable string used to represent the OLE application. It is a subkey of the object application's CLSID. It is also a key of the predefined HKEY_CLASSES_ROOT. HKEY_CLASSES_ROOT\ ProgID=<programmatic identifier>.

Like the CLSID key, the ProgID key contains many subkeys. These subkeys are described in the following subsections.

Insertable Key

HKEY_CLASSES_ROOT\ProgID\Insertable
This key indicates that the object is insertable into a container application.

Protocol Key

HKEY_CLASSES_ROOT\ProgID\ Protocol
This key indicates the protocol used by this ProgID. The protocol can contain the following subkey(s):

StdFileEditing // the object is insertable in OLE 1 containers

   Server = <full path to the server object>

   Verb

      0 = < verb 0>

      1 = <verb 1>

The StdFileEditing key contains a Server. Server specifies the full path to the OLE 2 object application. This information also can be used to display an object's icon if no icon is specified by any of the following keys: DefaultIcon, LocalServer, InprocServer, or InprocHandler.

CLSID Key

HKEY_CLASSES_ROOT\ProgID\ CLSID =<CLSID>
This key provides the conversion from ProgID to <CLSID>. Function CLSIDFromProgID provides the conversion from ProgID to CLSID.

Shell Key

HKEY_CLASSES_ROOT\ProgID\Shell

This key contains Windows 3.1 File Manager information. Its subkeys can be New, Print, PrintTo, and Open.

The TypeLib Key and Its Subkeys

The information associated with a type library can be found under the <TypeLib> key. <TypeLib> is the string representation of the UUID. One important piece of information stored under this key is the full path to the type library. The type library is used by the client to retrieve the data types of the properties and their methods in order to statically bind to the server object type. It stores the information for the data types for the properties, the return values, and the accepted parameters for the methods.

<TYPELIB> can contain the following possible subkeys:

Major.Minor = human readable string

  HelpDir = full path to the help file

  Flags = type library flag

  lcd

    win16 = <full path to the win16 platform type library>

    win32 = <full path to the win32 platform type library>

lcd is the string representation of the locale ID (lcid). The locale ID is a DWORD. The lower word contains a language identifier. The upper word contains a reserved value.

The Interface Key and Its Subkeys

HKEY_CLASSES_ROOT contains the Interface key. The subkeys for HKEY_CLASSES_ROOT\INTERFACE have the following form:

<IID> = <name of the interface>

The <IID> is a representation of the interface ID, which is of type UUID. The subkeys for each <IID> are listed next.

229

ProxyStubClsID Key

HKEY_CLASSES_ROOT\INTERFACE\<IID>\ProxyStubClsID = <CLSID>

This key maps an <IID> to a <CLSID>. It applies to the 16-bit proxy DLL, which is used for interprocess communication.

ProxyStubClsID32 Key

HKEY_CLASSES_ROOT\INTERFACE\<IID>\ ProxyStubClsID32= <CLSID>

This key maps an <IID> to a <CLSID> and applies only to 32-bit proxy DLLs.

NumMethods Key

HKEY_CLASSES_ROOT\INTERFACE\<IID>\ NumMethods = <number of methods in the interface>

This entry indicates the number of methods that the interface with <IID> supports.

BaseInterface Key

HKEY_CLASSES_ROOT\INTERFACE\<IID>\ BaseInterface = <IID>.

This key indicates the base interface from which the base interface is derived. Absence of this key means the base interface is IUnknown. If the key is present but without a value, then nothing is derived. For example, if your application adds a new interface, the <IID> key must be registered on the system. Each new interface on the system needs a single <IID> key.

To enumerate all the interfaces implemented by an object, first instantiate the object by invoking CoCreateInstance to retrieve a pointer to the IUnknown interface (pIUnknown). Using pIUnknown, then invoke pIUnknown -> QueryInterface(...) by trying every subkey <IID> under HKEY_CLASSES_ROOT\INTERFACE\. A successful call means the interface with the specified <IID> was implemented; otherwise, the interface with <IID> was not implemented.

The AppID Key and Its Subkeys

The Application Identifier (AppID) was introduced to hold the Distributed COM (DCOM) objects configuration information. The hierarchy of the AppID key is similar to that of the CLSID key. It is located under HKEY_CLASSES_ROOT\APPID\<AppID> = server name.

The possible name-value pairs for the <AppID> key are as follows:

Name: RemoteServerName
Value: <server name>

Name: ActivateAtStorage
Value: "Y"

Name: LaunchPermission
Value: <binary stream>

The latter binary stream describes the access control list (ACL). If the LaunchPermission name-value pair is not present, the COM library will retrieve the information listed below the key located at HKEY_LOCAL_MACHINE\SOFTWARE\MICROSOFT\OLE.

Name: DefaultLaunchPermission
Value: <binary stream>

Name: AccessPermission
Value: <binary stream>

The latter binary stream describes the access control list.
Note: The above Registry setting can be configured via tool dcomcnfg.exe. This tool is available when you install NT 4.0.

If you want to check whether your system has DCOM enabled, inspect the Registry entry HKEY_LOCAL_MACHINE\SOFTWARE\MICROSOFT\OLE and use the following name-value pair:

Name: EnableDCOM
Value: Y

If the value is Y, then the DCOM is supported under the current system. Otherwise, the DCOM is not supported.

The Component Category Key and Its Subkeys

The Component Category is used to categorize COM objects. Its key is located under HKEY_CLASSES_ROOT\Component Categories. It can contain the subkeys given in Table 6.2.

If your object class is a scripting engine, the Implemented Categories subkey should be created under its <CLSID>.

The Registry key entries for each <CLSID> within the Registry are very important in seamlessly integrating the various subtechnologies within ActiveX. Furthermore, any application that uses an ActiveX such as Internet information Server will also rely on the CLSID structure within the Registry. We cover this in the next section, where we discuss Microsoft's new Internet infrastructure solution, Internet Information Server.

Table 6.2 Component Category subkeys

Subkey	Name-Value	Meaning
40FC6ED3-2438-11CF-A3DB-080036F12502	409, OLE Embeddable objects	The old key for this is Insertable.
40FC6ED4-2438-11CF-A3DB-080036F12502	409, OLE Controls	The old key for this is Control.
40FC6ED5-2438-11CF-A3DB-080036F12502	409, OLE Automation objects	Programmable.
40FC6ED8-2438-11CF-A3DB-080036F12502	409, OLE Document objects	DocObject.
40FC6ED9-2438-11CF-A3DB-080036F12502	409, _Printable	Printable.
7DD95801-9882-11CF-9FA9-00AA006C42C4	409, Controls that are safely scriptable	Controls that are safely scriptable
7DD95802-9882-11CF-9FA9-00AA006C42C4	409, Controls safely initializable from persistent data	Controls safely initializable from persistent data
F0B7A1A1-9847-11CF-8F20-00805F2CD064	409, Active Scripting Engine	Active scripting engine
F0B7A1A2-9847-11CF-8F20-00805F2CD064	409, Active Scripting Engine with parsing	Active scripting engine with parsing

Internet Information Server and ActiveX Server Framework

Both the Internet Information Server (IIS) and the ActiveX Server Framework use the Registry extensively. IIS is a Hypertext Transfer Protocol (HTTP) Web server that runs on the Windows NT Server operating system version 3.51 or higher. It has four components: Internet Services, Internet Database Connector, Key Manager, and Internet Service Manager. The ActiveX Server Framework encompasses many of the extensions to the Microsoft Internet Information Server Side technologies. These extensions include the Internet Server Applications (ISA), the Internet Server Application Programming Interface Filters (ISAPI Filters), the Server Side controls, and Server Side scripting.

IIS has four components:

1. **Internet Services.** These services include a World Wide Web service to create a Web publishing service, a File Transfer Protocol (FTP) to transmit and receive files, and a Gopher service to publish archives of information.

2. **Internet Database Connector (IDC)** (httpodbc.dll). IDC is an Internet Server Application that uses 32-bit Open Database Connectivity (ODBC) to gain access to a variety of databases. The IDC sits between the Internet Server and the ODBC layer.

3. **Key Manager.** The Key Manager is used to install the Secure Socket Layer (SSL) keys.

4. **Internet Service Manager.** The Internet Service Manager is used to administer the Internet services.

The extensions that ActiveX Server Framework encompasses include these:

1. **Internet Server Application (ISA).** An ISA can be created to provide a high-performance client-server application. An ISA communicates with the HTTP server via an Extension Control Block (ECB), while a Common Gateway Interface (CGI) executable communicates with the server via environment variables.

2. **Internet Server Application Programming Interface Filters (ISAPI Filters).** An ISAPI filter is a replaceable DLL that is called by the HTTP server in response to a HTTP request. The filter tells the server what sort of notification (event) it will accept when it is first loaded by the server. After that, the filter is called on to process the event whenever a selected event occurs. An ISAPI filter can be created to listen to incoming and outgoing requests and automatically perform actions, such as custom authentication, compression, encryption, and enhanced logging.

An ISA or ISAPI filter is loaded at runtime into the HTTP server's own address space by using the function LoadLibrary. Because they share the same address space as the HTTP server process, they inherit access to the resources that are available to that server. The HTTP server also can decide when to unload these ISAPI DLLs.

IIS is a Microsoft application, so any application configuration and initialization data should be stored under the key HKEY_LOCAL_MACHINE\SOFTWARE\Company Name.

IIS Setup Registry Entries

When IIS is first installed, it creates setup Registry entries during the setup, as shown in Figure 6.4.

The figure shows three keys associated with the IIS setup Registry entries: INetMgr, INetStp, and INetExplore. All are stored under HKEY_LOCAL_MACHINE\SOFTWARE\Microsoft.

In the figure, the INetMgr key has a value called InstalledBy. This value indicates that IIS is installed on the system. INetMgr contains a subkey called Parameters, shown in Figure 6.5.

In Figure 6.5, the subkey Parameter's value—MajorVersion and MinorVersion—indicates the IIS version number. The version of IIS installed on this machine depicted in the figure is 2.0. The 2 stands for the major version; the 0 stands for the minor version.

In the figure, subkey Parameters also contains two subkeys: AddOnServices and AddOnTools. The AddOnServices key indicates the configuration DLL used by AddOnServices. There are three values for the AddOnServices key, as shown in Figure 6.6: FTP, Gopher, and WWW.

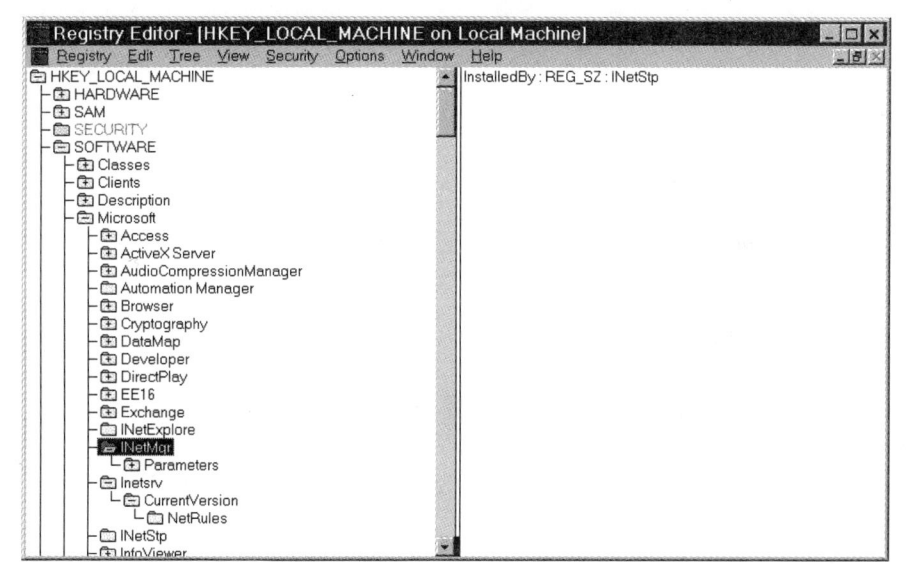

Figure 6.4 IIS setup Registry entries

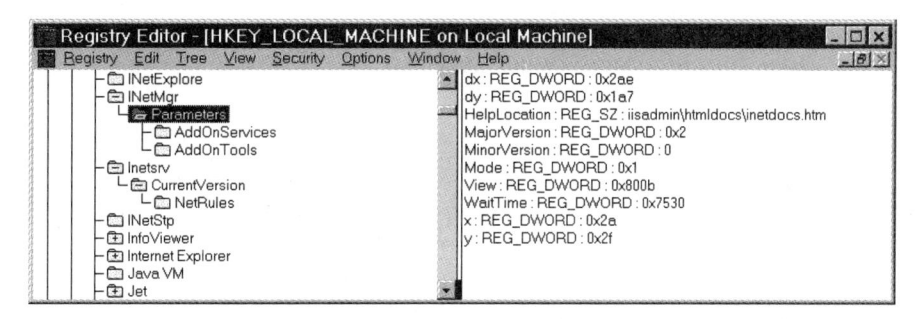

Figure 6.5 INetMgr Key and its subkeys

In the figure, value name FTP defines the configuration DLL (fscfg.dll) used by the FTP service. Value name Gopher defines the configuration DLL (gscfg.dll) used by the Gopher service. Value name WWW defines the configuration DLL (w3scfg.dll) used by the Web service.

The values of key INetStp are shown in Figure 6.7. In all these values, InstallPath indicates the directory in which IIS is installed. AnonymousUser indicates the anonymous user account created during the setup process.

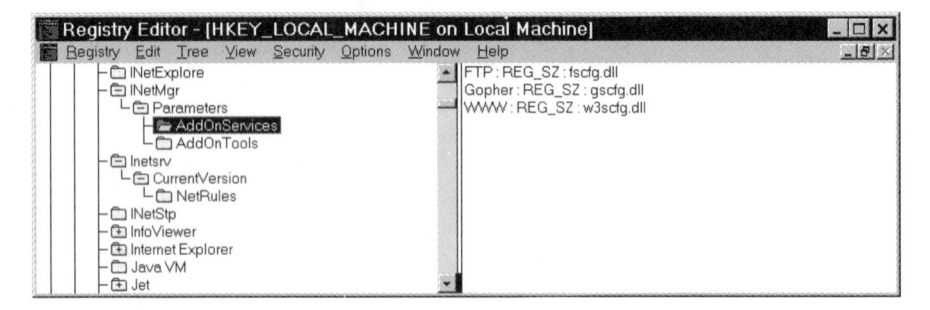

Figure 6.6 AddOnServices key

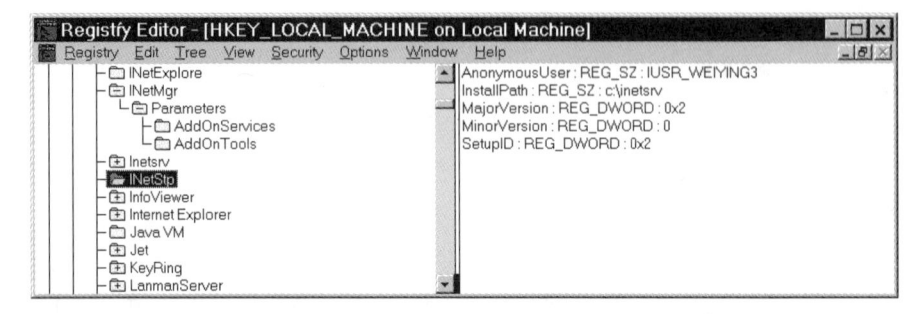

Figure 6.7 INetStp key and its values

The IIS setup Registry entries are used to determine the current configuration of IIS by the setup program after the initial setup.

IIS is a set of services. All NT services must register their information under key HKEY_LOCAL_MACHINE\SYSTEM\CurrentControlSet\ Services. All the service configuration and initialization information can be found under the root key Services, HKEY_LOCAL_MACHINE\SYSTEM\ CurrentControlSet\Services. For Services, three subkeys are created:

1. **Parameters.** Stores the service configuration and initialization data.

2. **Performance.** Stores the configuration data for the service's performance monitoring capabilities.

3. **Security.** Contains the security access information for the WWW service.

Keys specifically created for IIS are the following:

1. **INetInfo.** Stores the global control information of the Internet services.

2. **W3SVC.** Stores all the parameter and performance configuration / initialization data for the WWW service.

3. **GOPHERSVC.** Used for the Gopher service.

4. **MSFTPSVC.** Used for the FTP service.

INetInfo Registry Entries and Keys for ActiveX Programming

Figure 6.8 shows the INetInfo key and its subkeys. Notice that under INetInfo's Parameters key there is a key called MimeMap. MimeMap contains the default Multiple Internet Mail Extensions (MIME) mapping installed by IIS.

MIME Mapping

MIME mapping ensures that the server maps the file type correctly so that the browser can pick an appropriate application to present the data to the user. MIME type is always indicated in the content-type of the HTTP header.

The value name for the MimeMap key is defined in the following format:

<mime type/subtype>, <extension>, <unused>, <gopher item type>

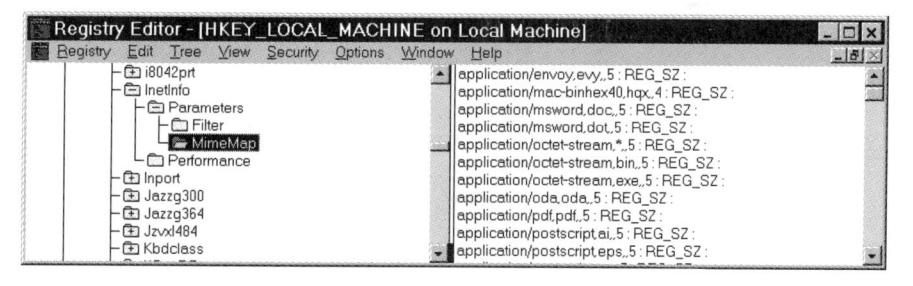

Figure 6.8 INetInfo key and its subkeys

Note that there is no value data associated with value names. The value type is always REG_SZ. For example, the value name

```
application/msword,doc,,5
```

indicates that the MIME type is an application and the subtype is msword.

Note: Besides the MIME type application, there are other MIME types such as audio, image, text, and x-world. These can be found in the value associated with the MimeMap key.

In the previous example, the application extension is .doc. The Gopher item type used by the Gopher server is specified with the integer 5. This means the msword document is an MS-DOS binary archive. Table 6.3 shows some of the Gopher item types and their meanings.

Table 6.3 Gopher item types

Type	Meaning
0	A file, which is always a flat text file.
1	A gopher directory.
2	A CSO phone-book server.
3	An error.
4	A Macintosh file.
5	An MS-DOS binary archive.
6	A UNIX file which is uuencoded.
7	A server for index searching.
8	A Telnet session.
9	A binary file.
c	A calendar or calendar of events.
g	A graphic interchange file (GIF) graphic.
h	An HTML page.
i	An in-line text that is not an item.
I	Another kind of image file.

In addition to using the default MIME mapping, you can specify a custom MIME mapping by following these steps, which will associate extension .tst with the test.exe application:

1. Start regedt32.exe and open HKEY_LOCAL_MACHINE\SYSTEM\ CurrentControlSet\Services\InetInfo\MimeMap.

2. From the Edit menu, choose Add Value.

3. Enter Application/test,tst,,5 for the value name and select the REG_SZ data type.

4. Click OK.

On the browser side, the association of application test.exe with the suffix .tst must be specified so that when the browser identifies the .tst suffix, it will invoke test.exe application.

WWW Service Registry Entries and Keys for ActiveX Programming

Figure 6.9 shows the W3SVC root key and its subkeys and values.

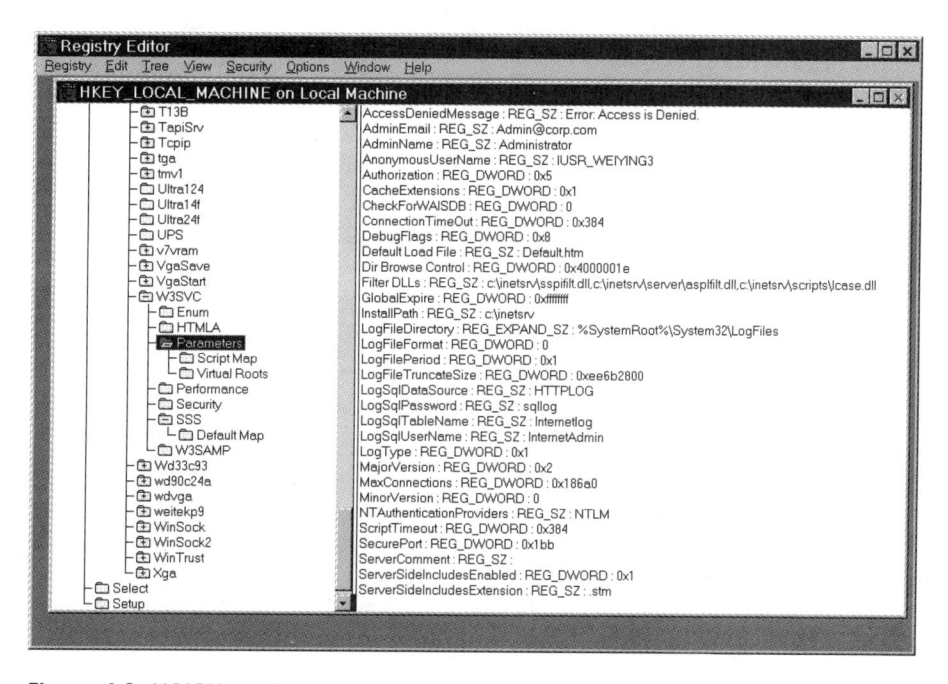

Figure 6.9 WWW service and its subkeys

The figure shows all the values for the Parameters key for the WWW service. Most Registry entries can be set using the Internet Service Manager. For example, suppose you want to change the log file directory and set the logging to weekly. Instead of changing the value LogFileDirectory and LogFilePeriod shown in the figure using regedt32, you can more easily use the Internet Service Manager, as follows:

1. Open the Microsoft Internet Service Manager.

2. Click the computer name on the WWW service line.

3. Select the Logging property sheet.

4. Click the "Weekly" radio button and change the log file directory to c:\temp, shown in Figure 6.10.

5. Click Apply.

The value for LogFileDirectory in the Registry will be changed to c:\temp. That for LogFilePeriod will be changed to 2, where 2 stands for weekly (1 stands for daily).

As you can see, using Internet Service Manager to configure the settings is much easier than changing the information directly in the Registry, a process that requires you to remember all the numbers' meanings.

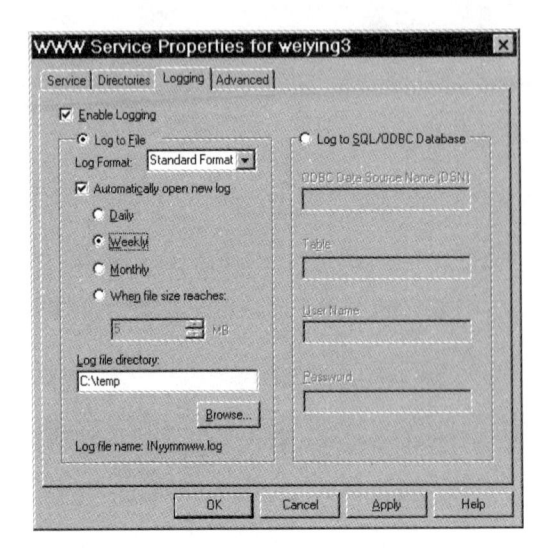

Figure 6.10 Internet Service Manager's logging property sheet

ScriptTimeout specifies the maximum time the WWW service will wait for a response from a CGI script. SecurePort specifies the TCP/IP port number used by the SSL.

ServerSideIncludesExtension specifies the extension, .stm, which is used by an HTML file, including other files with the include statement. The include statement in HTML allows you to add common information to every HTML page.

ISAPI Filter and FilterDlls Registry Values

The full path of the ISAPI Filter DLL must be added in the value FilterDlls so that the WWW service can locate and load the ISAPI filter DLL on demand. The following steps demonstrate how to add test.dll to the Registry so that the server can load it (assuming you have a filter called test.dll):

1. Compile the project.

2. Copy test.dll to the c:\inetsrv\scripts directory.

3. Start regedt32.exe and open HKEY_LOCAL_MACHINE\SYSTEM\ CurrentControlSet\Services\w3svc\parameters.

4. Double-click the FilterDlls value.

5. In the String edit box, enter c:\inetsrv\scripts\test.dll.

6. Click OK.

Note: If the key has filters listed, add a comma and your path to the end of the string. Remember, a comma, not a semicolon. For example, if there is a value in the filter DLLs, then , c:\netsrv\scripts\test.dll should be entered, not ; c:\netsrv\scripts\test.dll.

7. Restart the WWW service by opening the Control Panel and selecting the Services applet. In the Services dialog box, highlight World Wide Publishing service and click Stop. Then click Start to start the service.

Note: The service must be restarted (either by stopping the service and restarting it or by rebooting your computer) in order for the service to load your filter DLL.

For more information on ISAPI filters, check the Microsoft IIS documentation.

ISAPI Debugging and CacheExtensions Registry Value

If you want to force a reload of the extension DLLs each time they are used by the WWW service, you must set the value of the CacheExtensions to 0, as follows:

1. Start regedt32.exe and open HKEY_LOCAL_MACHINE\SYSTEM\ CurrentControlSet\Services\w3svc\parameters.

2. Double-click the CacheExtensions value.

3. In the DWORD edit box, enter 0.

4. Click OK.

These steps set the value data of HKLM\SYSTEM\CurrentControlSet\ Services\w3svc\Parameters\CacheExtensions to be 0. This setting will cause the server to reinitialize DLLs each time they are used. If this setting is 1, which is the default, the server will keep DLLs in memory as long as possible.

For more information on debugging Internet extension DLLs, see Visual C++ 4.x Technical Note 63.

Script Mapping Registry Keys

The key Parameters also has two subkeys in addition to the values for the Parameters shown in Figure 6.9: ScriptMap and VirtualRoots. Figure 6.11 shows the value associated with the ScriptMap subkey.

IIS uses the filename extension to determine which application is associated with the extension. The default application association is

```
.idc=c:\inetsrv\server\httpodbc.dll
```

This extension file mapping precludes the need to refer to httpodbc.dll in the URL. In other words, the server will map the .idc file to the httpodbc.dll.

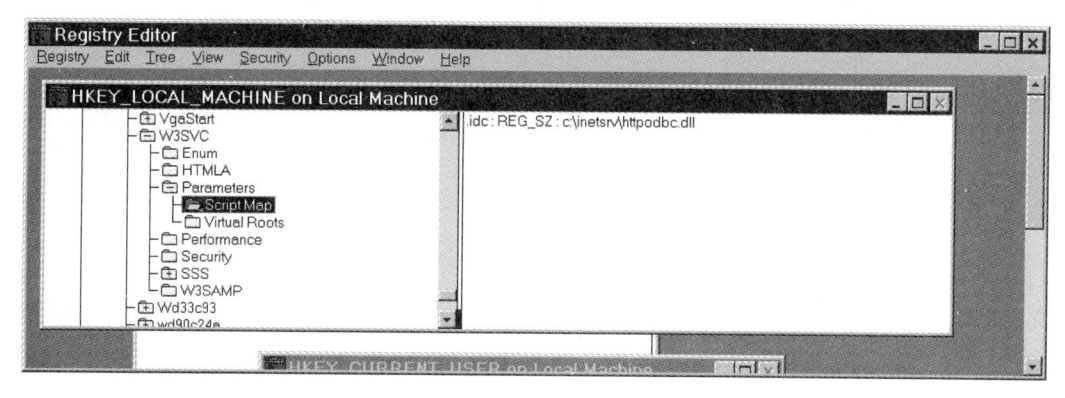

Figure 6.11 Value of the ScriptMap subkey

The IDC uses two types of files. One is the IDC file (.idc), which contains the information on how to connect to the ODBC data source and execute the SQL statement. The other is the HTML extension file (htx), which contains information on how the output Web page is constructed.

For instance, if the user types http://<server name>/test.idc, then when the server receives this URL, it will load the httpodbc.dll based on the test.idc file extension.

The following example describes how to create your own file extensions. Suppose the user types the URL http://<Server Name>/scripts/61.pl? and wants 61.pl to be associated with perl.exe. The script mapping can be created as follows:

1. Start regedt32.exe and open HKEY_LOCAL_MACHINE\SYSTEM\CurrentControlSet\Services\W3SVC\Parameters\ScriptMap.

2. From the Edit menu, choose Add Value.

3. Enter pl for the Value Name, select REG_SZ data type, and click OK.

4. In the String edit dialog box, type the full path to the interpreter, c:\perl.exe %s. perl.exe is under the root directory of the C drive.

5. Restart the WWW service.

The new value will be added as shown in Figure 6.12.

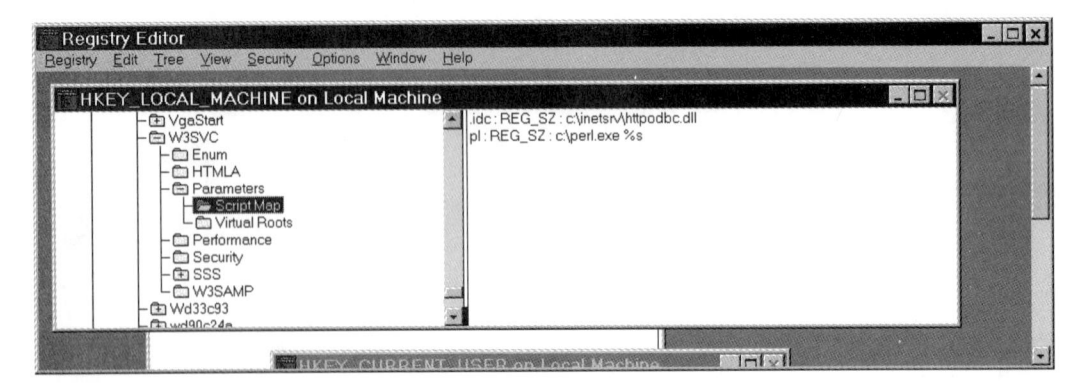

Figure 6.12 Custom script mapping

The following Perl script creates a sample "Hello World" that can be invoked as URL http://<server name>/scripts/61.pl. The sample 61.pl is given in Listing 6.1.

Listing 6.1
```
print "Content-Type: text/html\n";
print "<HTML>\n";
print "<HEAD>\n";
print "<TITLE>Script Mapping(Perl application and .pl
extension)</TITLE>\n";
print "</HEAD>\n";

print "<BODY>\n";
print "<H1>Hello World </H1>\n";
print "<P>\n";
print "<P>";
print "</BODY>\n";
print "</HTML>\n";
```

Since .pl extension is associated with perl.exe, the browser will display the "Hello World" string when a page with this extension is loaded. The 61.p1 example is quite simple when you think of how many more powerful operations are performed by some of the more complex ActiveX technologies. It is the Windows NT Registry that forms the infrastructure that allows so many types of applications, using such diverse technologies, to share and maintain information of all types.

Summary

The Registry is a key component to the Windows NT operating system and the support of many Microsoft technologies. A great deal of information is needed to support and integrate these technologies into a fairly seamless infrastructure. The CLSID, PROGID, and APPID are very important to the infrastructure of the ActiveX technologies, since ActiveX is based on the COM specification that uses the various identifiers to uniquely identify objects and obtain information on the object's capabilities.

Name-value pairs and subkeys offer a file system that resembles a hierarchy when accessing the Registry. This hierarchy allows for the maintenance of a great deal of information, as in the cases of the COM-based, OLE-based, and ActiveX technologies.

Chapter 7

NT Shell Extension Programming

NT shell extension programming is a way to customize the NT shell. Customizing the shell enables you as a programmer to influence how the shell works by allowing file objects of your design to have special abilities within the shell. In this chapter, we show you how to program the NT shell using shell extensions that both Windows NT and Windows 95 support.

The Shell

A **shell** is what most people consider to be the operating system. Think of it as a GUI to manipulate file objects that may or may not have a GUI. It is just an application that a user can use to control other applications, such as opening files, running programs, dragging filenames to copy or move files, and deleting files. It displays icons for each file and object and allows the user to view the properties of each object.

The shell can be extended by an OLE control that uses the shell interface. Shell extensions allow programmers to assign a different icon to each file, control context menus, design additional property pages, and determine how an object is copied. A shell extension is not built into the objects it is manipulating. Rather it is a separate object that extends the functionality of the operating system.

The Namespace

The shell is organized in the form of a **namespace.** A namespace is a replacement for the traditional directory structure that computer users have become so familiar with. In fact, this directory structure of hierarchical directories and files is so popular that many people cannot understand any other organization of computer components. In Windows 95 and Windows NT 4.0, however, Microsoft expanded the directory structure into the namespace. An example of a namespace is the Desktop. The Desktop is considered to be a folder. You can copy files into it, delete files from it, and create folders in it. However, the Desktop is not a directory that exists on a hard disk; it is a namespace.

A namespace is organized like a directory. However, it can contain more than files; for example, information about storage devices, printers, and network resources. Anything you can support with a shell extension can be put in a namespace.

Folders

A folder is much like a file system directory. It contains items that are in the shell's namespace. However, it may be something other than a directory. For example, a virtual folder is a special type of folder that is not a directory. Virtual folders usually contain objects that are not files; for example, remote computers, storage devices, the Desktop folder, the Control Panel, the Printers folder, the Fonts folder, the My Computer folder, and the Network Neighborhood folder.

A folder many contain other folders, thus building a hierarchical structure in the namespace. Anything in a folder is considered a file object. A file object can be a file or another type of object such as a Control Panel application or a printer. Each folder can contain only certain types of objects. For instance, the Printers folder may contain only printer objects; it may not contain files.

There is no limit to the types of folders that may be in the namespace, and any type of file object can be in a folder. Each folder is a component object model (COM) object. Each COM object is programmed to handle the file objects that reside in it. For instance, the Printers folder is programmed to add or remove a printer. The interface in the COM object that supports folders is called IShellFolder. When an object is placed within a folder, it binds to the folder, and when it is removed, it releases the folder.

The file system uses certain special file system folders to hold file system objects. These folders are not part of the main directory structure. For example, the file objects that are in the Desktop folder reside in a directory on the hard drive. The task bar associations are also kept in directories of system folders. The locations of special file system folders are stored in the Registry under HKEY_CURRENT_USER / Software / Microsoft / Windows / CurrentVersion / Explorer / Shell Folders.

Registering Commands

Some commands that can be invoked on file objects in a folder are supported by the folder. These commands include Send To, Cut, Copy, Paste, Create Shortcut, Delete, Rename, and Properties. Other commands, called *verbs*, are defined by the user in the Registry or are defined by the operating system when it is installed. A verb is independent of the language that the application understands. Examples of verbs that the user can define are Edit and Play. Examples of verbs that the system is responsible for are Open, Print, Find, and Explore. The system provides a menu command name and localization for each verb.

To add a user-defined verb, you register in the HKEY_CLASSES_ROOT key a subkey for the shell, a subkey for each verb, and a command subkey for each menu command name. For example, suppose you want to create a verb for the extension .htm that allows users to edit an HTML file in Notepad. The operating system on Windows NT 4.0 already has one verb registered for the .htm extension—Open—which starts up Internet Explorer 3.0 and opens the file with the .htm extension in Internet Explorer. To register another verb to the .htm extension, for example, Edit, here's what you do:

1. Use the Registry Editor to create a key with the verb name Edit under HKEY_CLASSES_ROOT\ htmlfile\shell.

2. Create another key under HKEY_CLASSES_ROOT\htmlfile\shell called Command.

3. In the Command key, set the default name-value pair to the command you want executed, as follows:

```
C:\WINNT\Notepad.exe %1
```

%1 indicates that each file instance with that extension has a different icon.

4. In any shell folder, right-click a file that has the .htm extension. Edit will be one of the options in the pop-up menu list.

5. Choose Edit to open the file in Notepad.

Each pop-up menu that is associated with an extension has a default verb. The default verb is the verb that gets called when the user double-clicks a file in Explorer. You can change the default verb, thus changing the action that occurs when a file is double-clicked. You assign the default verb by setting the default name-value pair of the shell key. For example, if you want Edit to be the default verb for the previous example, you set HKEY_CLASSES_ROOT\htmlfile\shell default name-value pair to Edit.

You also can assign the access key. By default, the shell assigns the first letter of the key name as the access key. However, to assign a different access key for the verb, place an ampersand (&) before the letter of the key name you want to be the access key. For example, to assign to the access key the letter d in Edit, from the previous example, you would enter E&dit for the default name-value pair of the Edit HKEY_CLASSES_ROOT\ htmlfile\shell\Edit.

You also can edit whether the letters of the verb are uppercase or lower-case. By default, the shell uppercases the first letter of the verb. To change a letter's case, you set the default name-value pair of the verb key. For example, from the previous example, you can set the verb from Edit to EDIT by setting the default name-value pair of HKEY_CLASSES_ROOT\ htmlfile\shell\Edit to EDIT.

More About Shell Extensions

There are two type of shell extensions:

1. Those for file extensions

2. Those associated with file operations such as move, copy, and rename

The shell extensions are associated with files as follows:

■ **Context menu handler.** Adds items to the context menu for a specific file object. The context menu is the menu seen when a user right-clicks a file object in the shell.

- **Icon handler.** Adds specific attributes of a file object to an icon. Without extending the shell, you can assign different icons to files that have the same extension.

- **Property sheet handler.** Adds pages to the property sheet dialog box that the shell displays for a file object.

- **Data handler.** Adds functionality to file objects that are being dragged out of the folder.

- **Drop objects.** Adds functionality to file objects that accept objects that are dropped into them.

The second type of shell extension are those associated with file operations such as move, copy, and rename, as follows:

- **Copy hook handler.** Called when a folder object is about to be copied, moved, deleted, or renamed. It can either allow or prevent the operation.

- **Drag and drop handler.** A context menu handler that the system calls when the user drops an object after dragging it to a new position.

To implement a shell extension, you write a OLE COM object that resides as a DLL. The DLL implements the interfaces need for each handler. To attach the DLL to the shell, you register the COM object.

Overriding Icons with the Icon Handler

In Windows NT 4.0 and Windows 95, the shell uses icons next to the name of each file object in the namespace. Usually each file object is assigned an icon based on its extension. An icon handler can override the icon being displayed. In this way, files with the same extension can have different icons. An icon handler also can specify icons for folders and subfolders within the application's file structure.

An application can specify icons in either of two ways:

1. Specify a class icon to be used for files that have a particular extension.

2. Use an icon handler.

The easiest way is to specify a class icon for files that have a particular extension. You do this by adding a key to the Registry called DefaultIcon. This key is added under program information key. An application also can use a %1 with the DefaultIcon key.

The second way an application can specify icons is with an icon handler. An application may have only one icon handler. The icon handler's properties are added under the shellex key. The IconHandler entry points to the class identifier of the COM object that is handling the icon.

An icon handler must implement the IExtractIcon interface in order for the system to display an icon. Here are the steps followed:

1. Retrieves the class identifier of the handler from the Registry key IconHandler.

2. Creates a COM object using the class identifier and CoCreateInstance.

3. Initializes the instance by calling IPersistFile::Load.

4. Uses QueryInterface to get the IExtractIcon::Extract member function.

5. Calls IExtractIcon::GetIconLocation.

6. Calls IExtractIcon::Extract.

The shell calls the GetIconLocation member to get the location of the icon to display. Usually the icon location is the full path to either an executable or a DLL. In this case, the GetIconLocation member function returns an index into the DLL or executable so that the icon location can be found.

The Extract member function is called only when the shell needs to display an icon that does not reside in an executable or a DLL. If the icon is in a DLL or an executable, implementing this function simply returns E_FAIL. If the icon exists in any other format, for instance, an .ico file, then the Extract member function must extract the icon from the format and return its member function.

Handling the Context Menu

A context menu handler modifies the contents of the context menu. The context menu is the menu you see after you right-click a file object. Usually the context menu contains items such as Open and Properties. You also see a context menu when you drag a file object while holding down the right mouse button. In this case, the menu actions that affect the object you selected appear. A context menu assumes that files with the same file types (same file extensions) require the same actions.

When the right mouse button is clicked on a file object, the shell creates a default context menu for the selected object. The file object can be a file, folder, drive, or any other type of file object. The shell also calls all the context menu handlers that are registered for that type of file object.

There can be more than one context menu handler for any file object, and each one gets to add menu selections to the menu. The context menu handler COM object implements IContextMenu to add menu items to the context menu. The handler can implement the menu item in two ways. Either the menu item can be made specific to the file object; thus all file objects of a certain type have the same context menu. Or the context menu handler can add menu items on a per-instance basis. For example, different files would have different menus even if they are of the same file type.

When the user right-clicks the file object, the system passes the address of the object's default menu handlers to the context menu handler. The context menu handler then uses the address to add items to the menu. The context menu handler should only add items to the context menu; it should not modify or delete items from the menu. This is because there may be many context menu handlers being called for a particular file object and they can be called in any order. Also, the shell adds items after all the context menu handlers have been called. In this case, the menu item you want to delete might not exist. If multiple context menu handlers are registered for a particular file object, then the value of the key determines the order in which the menu items are inserted into the context menu. The key's value is determined by the order in which the subkeys were created in the ContextMenuHandler key.

When the user selects a menu item added by a context menu handler, the shell calls the handler's IContextMenu::InvokeCommand menu function. The handler then can process the menu function. Listing 7.1 shows an example of InvokeCommand.

Listing 7.1

```
STDMETHODIMP
CExampleExt::InvokeCommand(LPCMINVOKECOMMANDINFO lpcmi)
{
HRESULT hr = E_INVALIDARG;
```

```
if (!HIWORD(lpcmi->lpVerb)) {
UINT idCmd = LOWORD(lpcmi->lpVerb);

switch (idCmd)
{
case 0: // One and Only Menu Item
hr = HandlingFunction(lpcmi->hwnd, lpcmi->lpDirectory,
lpcmi->lpVerb, lpcmi->lpParameters, lpcmi->nShow);
break;
}
return hr;
}
```

When the shell wants to display a context menu, it calls the QueryContextMenu member function. To insert each menu item into the context menu, the context menu handler calls InsertMenu on the context menu. Listing 7.2 shows an example of QueryContextMenu.

Listing 7.2

```
STDMETHODIMP CExampleExt::QueryContextMenu(
HMENU hMenu,
UINT indexMenu,
UINT idCmdFirst,
UINT idCmdLast,
UINT uFlags)
{
UINT idCmd = idCmdFirst;
char szMenuText[21];

BOOL bAppendItems=TRUE;

if ((uFlags & 0x000F) == CMF_NORMAL) {
lstrcpy(szMenuText, "Do this to that");
} else if (uFlags & CMF_VERBSONLY) {
lstrcpy(szMenuText, "Do this to Shortcut");
} else if (uFlags & CMF_EXPLORE) {
lstrcpy(szMenuText, "Do this in Explorer");
} else if (uFlags & CMF_DEFAULTONLY) {
```

```
bAppendItems = FALSE;
} else {
char szTemp[32];
bAppendItems = FALSE;
}

if (bAppendItems) {

InsertMenu(hMenu, indexMenu++, MF_SEPARATOR |
MF_BYPOSITION, 0, NULL);

InsertMenu(hMenu, indexMenu++, MF_STRING |
MF_BYPOSITION, idCmd++, szMenuText);

InsertMenu(hMenu, indexMenu++, MF_SEPARATOR |
MF_BYPOSITION, 0, NULL);

// Must return the number of menu items added.
return ResultFromShort(idCmd-idCmdFirst);
}
return NOERROR;
}
```

The GetCommandString member function is called to get a language-independent command string or the help text for a context menu. Language-independent strings allow you to write context menu handlers that can be localized. The help text is displayed when a user uses the What's This? help pointer on the context menu handler's menu item.

Implementing Drag and Drop

The drag-and-drop menu that is displayed when you drag and drop while holding down the right mouse button is also implemented through IContextMenu. This menu is handled by drag-and-drop handlers. These handlers work like a context menu handler and should be registered under DataHandler in the folders file object type instead of being registered under each individual file object.

Modifying the Property Sheet

A property sheet handler is a COM object that adds a page to a file object's property sheet. A file object may have more than one property sheet handler, so multiple property sheets may be added, up to 24. When the user selects a file's properties, the shell displays a standard property sheet. If the file object has registered property sheet handlers, those property sheets are displayed also. Property sheet handlers implement the IShellPropSheetExt interface so that they can interact with the shell.

To register a property sheet handler, you create a key called PropertySheetHandlers under the shellex key in the Registry. The property sheet key names determine their order.

When the shell is about to display the property sheet, it calls AddPages on each registered property sheet handler. The property sheet handlers add property pages to the sheets. These pages are subclassed so that all their functionality is stored with the page.

Listing 7.3 shows an example of AddPages.

Listing 7.3

```
STDMETHODIMP CExampleExt::AddPages(LPFNADDPROPSHEETPAGE
lpfnAddPage, LPARAM lParam)
{
PROPSHEETPAGE psp;
HPROPSHEETPAGE hpage;

psp.dwSize       = sizeof(psp);    // no extra data
psp.dwFlags      = PSP_USEREFPARENT |
                   PSP_USERELEASEFUNC;
psp.hInstance    = (HINSTANCE)g_hmodThisDll;
psp.pszTemplate  = MAKEINTRESOURCE(DLG_FSPAGE);
psp.pfnDlgProc   = FSPage_DlgProc;
psp.pcRefParent  = &g_cRefThisDll;
psp.pfnRelease   = FSPage_ReleasePage;
psp.lParam       = (LPARAM)hdrop;

hpage = CreatePropertySheetPage(&psp);
if (hpage) {
if (!lpfnAddPage(hpage, lParam))
```

```
DestroyPropertySheetPage(hpage);
}
return NOERROR;
}
```

Replacing Control Panel Pages

Another member function, ReplacePage, allows the property pages of a Control Panel application to be replaced by custom property pages. Located in the IShellPropSheetExt interface, ReplacePage is called only by Control Panel applications, not by the shell. (The shell has no property pages that should be replaced.) Other property page handlers can use this function to replace property pages of different handlers.

For each property sheet handler that allows its property pages to be replaced, you need to define a key in the Registry where other property page handlers can register. These registered property page handlers replace the property pages for the first handlers. The key location is defined by REGSTR_PATH_CONTROLSFOLDER in regstr.h. For Windows NT 4.0, the location is Software\\Microsoft\\Windows\\CurrentVersion\\Controls Folder.

Within this key is an application name key that is a parent of the shellex key that has a PropertySheetHandlers key. An example of the PropertySheetHandlers key is the Microsoft Plus pack, which adds the following key to override the display properties in the Control Panel: HKEY_LOCAL_MACHINE\SOFTWARE\Microsoft\Windows\CurrentVersion\Controls Folder\Display\shellex\PropertySheetHandlers\PlusPack CPL Extension.

A property sheet handler also must define identifiers for each page that can be replaced. The identifiers allow other property page handlers to replace only the pages they want.

Copy Hook Handler

A copy hook handler verifies the moving, copying, deleting, or renaming of a file object. You can write copy hook handlers so that certain files cannot be manipulated from the shell. For example, you could write a copy hook handler that doesn't allow certain types of files to be deleted or a certain instance of a particular type of file.

The copy hook handler is called by the shell before a folder object is copied, moved, deleted, or renamed. The handler does not perform the operation; it only approves or disapproves it. A file object can have multiple copy hook handlers and each handler for that object must approve the operation. Once the shell gets approval from all the copy hook handlers, it performs the operation.

A copy hook handler COM object has one member function, CopyCallBack, which is implemented through IShellExitInt. CopyCallBack returns an integer indicating whether the operation should be performed. The first copy hook handler to return IDCANEL stops the shell from querying the rest of the handlers. If a copy hook handler approves the operation, the function should return IDYES; otherwise it should return IDNO.

Data Handlers

When a file is dragged from the shell or copied from the Clipboard, the shell creates an IDataObject interface. This interface supports standard Clipboard formats. Data handlers allow you to add more Clipboard formats to a particular file object that is being dragged. For a Data handlers interface to be added, the data handler must support the IDataObject interface. IDataObject calls the IDataObject interface in the data handler when the file is dragged and dropped, thus allowing the data handler to add the Clipboard formats.

Drop Handler

By default you cannot drag and drop a file object into another file. But you can enable this facility by writing a drop handler for the file object into which you want to drop the other file. For instance, you could write a drop handler that allows you to drop a text file into notepad.exe.

To implement a drop handler, you need to register the drop handler and support the IDropTarget interface. When a file object is dropped into the file object that has the registered drop handler, the IDropTarget interface is called.

Registering Shell Extensions

You must register in the HKEY_ CLASSES_ROOT key the COM object shell handler for each shell extension. Each COM object has a globally unique class identifier (GUID). For example, the shell extension has a GUID of {88B9BD00-F65C-11BD-A259-00DD010E8C26}. Registering the COM object creates a key out of the HKEY_ CLASSES_ROOT with the GUID that is the same as the key's name.

You also must mark the shell extension as "approved." To do this, you add a name-value pair to HKEY_LOCAL_MACHINE\SOFTWARE\ Microsoft\Windows\CurrentVersion\Shell Extensions\Approved. Here, the name of the name-value pair is the GUID of the COM object and the value is the ProgID.

You also need to create a unique extension for the file object type out of HKEY_CLASSES_ROOT. For example, suppose you want to create an extension type called .wwb. You have a key called HKEY_CLASSES_ ROOT\.wwb. Here's what you would do:

1. For the default name-value pair of that key, assign a unique name as the type of the file object. For this example, make the name Chapter 7 Example. Assign the default name-value pair of HKEY_CLASSES_ ROOT\.wwb to Chapter 7 Example.

2. Create another key under the HKEY_CLASSES_ROOT root with the name of the file object type; for example, HKEY_CLASSES_ROOT\ Chapter 7 Example.

3. In HKEY_CLASSES_ROOT\Chapter 7 Example, create a subkey called shellex.

4. In shellex, create other keys that identify the shell extension handler for the new file object. For example, create the key HKEY_CLASSES_ ROOT\Chapter 7 Example\shellex.

Registering the Icon Handler

To register a single icon handler, you create a subkey in shellex called IconHandler. Set the default name-value pair of IconHandler to the GUID of the COM object that is handling the icons. For the example, create a key called HKEY_CLASSES_ROOT\Chapter 7 Example\shellex\IconHandler and set the default name-value pair to {88B9BD00-F65C-11BD-A259-00DD010E8C26}.

When registering an icon handler for providing per-instance icons for a file object, set the value for the DefaultIcon key in HKEY_CLASSES_ROOT\Chapter 7 Example to %1.

Registering the Data Handler

To register a single data handler, you create a subkey in shellex key called DataHandler. Set the default name-value pair of DataHandler to the GUID of the COM object that is handling the icons. For the example, create a key called HKEY_CLASSES_ROOT\Chapter 7 Example\shellex\DataHandler and set the default name-value pair to {88B9BD00-F65C-11BD-A259-00DD010E8C26}.

A file object may have more than one data handler. To register multiple data handlers, create a key called HKEY_CLASSES_ROOT\Chapter 7 Example\shellex\DataHandler, just as you did for a single handler, but do not assign a default name-value pair. Then create multiple subkeys. Each subkey should be a different data handler and have a default name-value pair that has the GUID of the COM object that is the data handler. Each data handler will be able to handle the data.

Registering the Context Menu Handler

For the context menu handler, you create a subkey in shellex called ContextMenuHandlers and set the default name-value pair to Menu. For the example, create a key called HKEY_CLASSES_ROOT\Chapter 7 Example\shellex\ContextMenuHandlers.

Next create a subkey in ContextMenuHandlers called Menu. Assign the default name-value pair to the GUID of the COM object that is handling the context menu. For the example, you would create a key called HKEY_CLASSES_ROOT\Chapter 7 Example\shellex\ContextMenu Handlers\Menu and set the default name-value pair to {88B9BD00-F65C-11BD-A259-00DD010E8C26}.

A file object may have more than one context menu handler. To register multiple context menu handlers, create a key called HKEY_CLASSES_ ROOT\Chapter 7 Example\shellex\ContextMenuHandlers, just as you did for a single handler, but do not assign a default name-value pair. Then create multiple subkeys. Each subkey should be a different context handler and have a default name-value pair that has the GUID of the COM object that is the context handler. Each context handler will be able to add a portion to the context menu. An example of multiple context menus can be seen with the folders file object: HKEY_CLASSES_ROOT\Folder\shellex\ContextMenuHandlers.

Registering the Property Sheet Handler

To register the property sheet handler, you create a subkey in shellex called PropertySheetHandlers. Set the default name-value pair to Page. For the example, you would create a key called HKEY_CLASSES_ROOT\Chapter 7 Example\shellex\PropertySheetHandlers.

Next create a subkey in the PropertySheetHandlers key called Page. Assign the default name-value pair to the GUID of the COM object that is handling the property sheet menu. For the example, you would create a key called HKEY_CLASSES_ROOT\Chapter 7 Example\shellex\PropertySheetHandlers\Page and set the default name-value pair to {88B9BD00-F65C-11BD-A259-00DD010E8C26}.

A file object type can have more than one property page handler. To register multiple property page handlers, create a key called HKEY_CLASSES_ROOT\Chapter 7 Example\shellex\PropertySheetHandlers, just as you did for a single handler, but do not assign a default name-value pair. Then create multiple subkeys. Each subkey should be a different property page handler and have a default name-value pair that has the GUID of the COM object that is the property page handler. Each page handler will be able to add a property page to the context menu. An example of multiple property pages can be seen with the folders file object: HKEY_CLASSES_ROOT\Folder\shellex\PropertySheetHandlers.

Registering the Copy Hook Handler

To register the copy hook handler, you create a subkey in shellex called CopyHookHandlers. Set the default name-value pair to Hook. For the example, you would create a key called HKEY_CLASSES_ROOT\Chapter 7 Example\shellex\CopyHookHandlers.

Next create a subkey in CopyHookHandlers called Hook. Assign the default name-value pair to the GUID of the COM object that is handling the property sheet menu. For the example, you would create a key called HKEY_CLASSES_ROOT\Chapter 7 Example\shellex\CopyHookHandlers\Hook and set the default name-value pair to {88B9BD00-F65C-11BD-A259-00DD010E8C26}.

A file object may have more then one copy hook handler. To register multiple copy hook handlers, create a key called HKEY_CLASSES_ROOT\Chapter 7 Example\shellex\CopyHookHandlers, just as you did for a single handler, but do not assign a default name-value pair.

Then create multiple subkeys. Each one should be a different copy hook handler and have a default name-value pair that has the GUID of the COM object that is the copy hook handler. Each copy hook handler will be able to add a hook to the file object. An example of multiple copy hook handlers can be seen with the directories file object: HKEY_CLASSES_ROOT\Directory\shellex\CopyHookHandlers

Registering a Handler for All File Objects

To register a handler for all file objects, you create a shellex under the * key in HKEY_CLASSES_ROOT. Add the file handler keys, just as you would if you had a specific file object type. For the previous example, instead of adding IconHandler to HKEY_CLASSES_ROOT\Chapter 7 Example\shellex, you can add it to HKEY_CLASSES_ROOT*\shellex. All the file objects will use the GUID pointed to by IconHandler.

How the Shell Accesses Shell Extension Handlers

The shell uses two interfaces to initialize the shell extensions: IShellExitInit and IPersistFile. IShellExitInit is used to initialize instances of the context menu handlers, drag-and-drop handlers, and property sheet handlers. IPersistFile is used to initialize icon handlers, data handlers, and drop handlers.

IShellExitInit needs an extra member function called Initialize. Initialize is exposed through IUnknown. Listing 7.4 shows how to write the Initialize function so that it keeps a copy of the passed parameters for later use.

Listing 7.4

```
STDMETHODIMP CShellHander::Initialize(LPCITEMIDLIST
pIDFolder, LPDATAOBJECT DataObj, HKEY hRegKey)
{
// Initialize can be called more than once.
if (m_pDataObj)
m_pDataObj->Release();

// Save the object pointer.
if (pDataObj) {
m_pDataObj = pDataObj;
pDataObj->AddRef();
}

// Duplicate the Registry handle.
if (hRegKey)
RegOpenKeyEx(hRegKey, NULL, 0L, MAXIMUM_ALLOWED,
&this->hRegKey);

return NOERROR;
}
```

Every shell extension must implement these functions: DllMain, DllCanUnloadNow, and DllGetClassObject. DllCanUnloadNow and DllGetClassObject are the same for a shell extension as for any other OLE in-process (in-proc) server. As is usual in most cases, DllGetClassObject needs to expose the class Factory for the object in the DLL.

INDEX

Numbers followed by the letter f indicate figures; numbers followed by the letter t indicate tables.

A

Access key, designating, 250
ActiveX, overview of, 213–215
ActiveX controls, 214
  registering and unregistering, 166–167, 214–215, 215f
ActiveX scripting, 214
ActiveX Server Framework, 233
AddOnServices key, 234, 236f
AddOnTools key, 234
AddPages function, 256–257
advapi32.dll, 131
APIs
  in C++ applications, 163–212
  described, 132
  listed, 41–130
  in Visual Basic applications, 131–161
AppID key, 227
  subkeys of, 231
Array of strings data type, 3
AuxUserType key, 223

B

Backup key, defined, 50–51
Backups
  restoring, 10–11
  in Windows 95, 10
  in Windows NT, 10
Backward slash, 1–2, 44
BaseInterface key, 230
Binary data, 3
  changing value of, 23, 24f
Binary values, declaring, 37–38

Boolean data type, 139
ByRef, 140
Byte data type, 139
ByVal, 140

C

C++, API use in, 163–212
  pointers in, 146–147
Case sensitivity, 139
Close name-value pair, 188
CLSID key, 216–217, 226
  as subkey of ProgID, 228
  subkeys of, 217–227
Collect name-value pair, 189
Commands, registering, 249–250
Common Gateway Interface (CGI), 233
Component Category key, 232
  subkeys of, 232t
Component Object Model, 214
Context menu, 252
  displaying, 253–254
  selecting item on, 252–253
Context menu handler, 250
  registering, 260–261
ContextMenuHandler key, 253
Control key, 219
Control panel, replacing pages on, 257
Conversion key, 225
Copy hook handler, 251, 257–258
  registering, 261–262
CopyCallBack function, 258
Counter, defined, 185
Creating a key, 17–18, 18f, 19f, 35
  APIs for, 47–54
  in C, 140–144
  in Visual Basic, 144–148
Currency data type, 139
CurVer key, 226